Tim was a Northern Michigan resident who recently transplanted himself to the Chicagoland area. Tim received his BS in English from Central Michigan University in 2005. He is a writer, singer/songwriter, musician, teacher, and former elected official. He moved to Illinois to be closer to his daughter.

Timothy G. Schaiberger

A BOY SCOUT GOES TO SPAIN… AND OTHER STORIES

AUSTIN MACAULEY PUBLISHERS™
LONDON • CAMBRIDGE • NEW YORK • SHARJAH

Copyright © Timothy G. Schaiberger 2023

All rights reserved. No part of this publication may be reproduced, distributed, or transmitted in any form or by any means, including photocopying, recording, or other electronic or mechanical methods, without the prior written permission of the publisher, except in the case of brief quotations embodied in critical reviews and certain other non-commercial uses permitted by copyright law. For permission requests, write to the publisher.

Any person who commits any unauthorized act in relation to this publication may be liable to criminal prosecution and civil claims for damages.

All of the events in this memoir are true to the best of the author's memory. The views expressed in this memoir are solely those of the author.

Ordering Information
Quantity sales: Special discounts are available on quantity purchases by corporations, associations, and others. For details, contact the publisher at the address below.

Publisher's Cataloging-in-Publication data
Schaiberger, Timothy G.
A Boy Scout Goes to Spain… and Other Stories

ISBN 9798889100270 (Paperback)
ISBN 9798889100287 (ePub e-book)

Library of Congress Control Number: 2023909859

www.austinmacauley.com/us

First Published 2023
Austin Macauley Publishers LLC
40 Wall Street, 33rd Floor, Suite 3302
New York, NY 10005
USA

mail-usa@austinmacauley.com
+1 (646) 5125767

I would like to dedicate this book to my father and grandfather. They both lived such interesting lives. They were both taken far too soon from me and I miss them terribly. I am honored to be able to tell their stories to people.

Table of Contents

Context	9
Time for Some More Context	74
Part 2: A Surgeon Goes to War	75
Part 3: The Son Soon Follows	98
References	105

Context

I thought I knew a lot about my family and our shared history, but I was unaware of so much. That is why I was shocked and pleasantly surprised by what I discovered when I was 22. This was before Ancestry.com and all the varied interest in family histories.

I was cleaning out the basement at my parents' house a few months after my father died (due to a Glioblastoma Multiforme [malignant brain tumor] from exposure to Agent Orange during his service in Vietnam) and I found an old wooden footlocker. It had always been on the top of the glass-door gun case in the corner of the room and I never really paid it any heed. But, on this particular day, I took it down and I opened it. What I found inside was a wonderful discovery…

The footlocker was full of correspondence, pictures, and artifacts from my grandfather's past. I didn't know that this treasure trove of family history existed. My father must have inherited it from him. It had been well over a decade since my grandfather had died from heart disease, but he still brought back fond memories from those who knew him. The reputation of my grandfather was known throughout the county. He even has his own chapter in the county book of lore.

I began to look through the collection that lay before me. There was a batch of classified World War II pictures of surgeries, surgical techniques, and bombing sites. Another group of pictures showed military conviviality between soldiers. I also noticed an undeveloped roll of film which, at its 70-year storage rate, would probably be unsalvageable.

I then encountered, folded up and secured with a rusty paper clip, a typed presentation of last rights to give for dying soldiers (with an annotated religious affiliation consideration, i.e., Catholic, Protestant, Jewish). There was an ancient M-80, various pins, awards, medals, and a military discharge paper signed by Harry Truman.

There was a book of Boy Scout cards and a cigar box full of Boy Scout and military patches. I remembered some stories about my grandfather that he almost made Eagle Scout, but he was never a strong enough swimmer. He never got that badge.

Next to the cigar box, stuffed under the 6 June 1944 issue of the *Toledo Blade* claiming 'Allies Invade North France in Landings by Air and Sea: Battle raging 10 miles from coast, Nazis say,' I noticed the rounded edge of a small book.

It was plain brown and bore no title on the binding. I pulled it out and the little book only had "My Trip" written in gold lettering in the top left corner. I thought that was an unusual name for a book until I opened it and read:

George L. Schaiberger 450 Waggoner Blvd. Toledo, Ohio.

On the second page, it read:

Going May 17–1934 Toledo, Spain. It is a mild, nice sunny morning.
A good place to eat in Madrid is Heidelberg Restaurant, Madrid, near the Chamber of Deputies.

As I turned each page, I started to discover an unknown-to-me part of my family history.

This is my grandfather's story.

In 1934, my 16-year-old grandfather was a dedicated and hardworking Boy Scout in Toledo, Ohio, and a student in Mr. Russell Brown's Spanish class at DeVilbiss High School. Although he would go on to be the President of the Student Senate at DeVilbiss High School, as well as graduating first in his class, he actually was not the top Spanish student in Mr. Brown's class. The top student in line for this opportunity had fallen ill and my grandfather took his place. He was chosen to be a part of a delegation initially called *The Committee on Relations with Toledo, Spain.* It was the first visit of what was to be eventually dubbed The Association of Two Toledos.

The Delegation-Association of Two Toledos:

This is an image of the members of the Toledo, Ohio, delegation to Toledo, Spain. They are listed as follows: front row left to right: Mrs. Stephen K. Mahon; Vice-Mayor Charles D. Hoover; Mrs. Grove Patterson; back row left to right: George Schaiberger, Spanish student and student body president of DeVilbiss High School (my grandfather); Dr. Henry Doermann, President of Toledo University (as it was then known); Stephen K. Mahon, President of the Managing Board of Toledo University; Russel G. C. Brown, Spanish teacher at DeVilbiss H.S.; and Grove Patterson, editor of the Toledo Blade newspaper.

This affluent group of travelers embarked on a journey through New York, France, Spain, and Morocco together.

This is my grandfather's personal journal, recording the events of the trip and all of his adventures. You will read about bus accidents, hotel room robberies, sea travel, Spanish bullfights, and the habits of North African Moors. These stories and more await you in these recollections.

He saw and experienced the most fantastic things. He traveled to a land with history and traditions centuries older than his own and stood in awe of the customs and daily life of these people. He learned so much and I assume he always held these memories close.

I didn't know of this story before I found his journal. My grandfather died when I was 13. We were close but he never spoke of this experience with me. I remember as a child, after he had retired with my grandmother and they moved to Arizona, he would speak Spanish with the local populace. That was just a passing thing at that time because I was a kid and didn't know any better.

In my research for this project, I was able to get in contact with the son of Russel G.C. Brown, Russel C. Brown. We met for lunch and he was able to help me fill in the blank spaces and helped me translate some Spanish quotes and autographs. He was indispensable in the research process of this project; unfortunately, he also passed away before I was finished. I hope he would have been proud of the outcome.

A day-by-day recollection of a 1930s American teenager's experiences in Europe and North Africa is a new look into history. This journal gives an in depth view of pre-civil war Spain seen through the eyes of a live witness, experiencing different cultures and being motivated, not only by youthful exuberance, but with the eye of an unwitting cultural anthropologist. I hope that this will one day be read by people who want to learn more about Spain in the run-up to the civil war. To see how the world of the upper class differentiated greatly from that of the average person, let alone the poorest. This journal shows how a world travel experience can lay the foundation for a successful life. If you're lucky and can afford it, that is.

This journal is transcribed below as close to the original, hand-written form as possible, to properly relate some of his chicken scratch. These lines have been edited for clarity and contain references and themes that might be found questionable today. But I chose to keep everything as is to show the reality of the time. The journal begins with my grandfather taking the train from Toledo to New York City...

May 17th 1934, Thursday

On the train from Toledo to New York

I left Toledo, Ohio, for New York at 5:20pm. We went through Cleveland on the way out and I had my first meal in a dining car. I slept in the chair seat. There was a BIG farewell at the train station to see us off, with many photographers.

May 18th 1934, Friday

New York City

We traveled along the Hudson River Valley on our way east and there was a beautiful background of high-red rock. We went through many different subways and I saw a mast-ship. We stopped to check in at the Roosevelt Hotel.

The subways here are very crowded.

I walked on Wall St. and I saw Radio City Music Hall and J.P. Morgan's office building.

We went past Trinity Church and I saw the graves of Alexander Hamilton and Robert Fulton. The church is located in the center of the city. After we visited the church, we went to the Spanish and French counsels for visas. There are so many cabs here. They are everywhere.

May 19th 1934, Saturday

New York to Havre, France

We left from New York on the SS "Paris" to Havre, France.

I got together my introduction letters from the Mayor of Toledo and the Governor of Ohio and I finally got to see Times Square. We rode a taxi to the pier and the boat we were taking, sure was large.

There were five photographers taking our pictures on deck. I saw my cabin and it sure is swell. Out of my stateroom window I saw Einstein among the crowd. (This could have been the actual Albert Einstein himself, as he moved to New York with his wife in 1933.)

I ate my first meal on the boat at 1:15. There was a large crowd at the pier to see us off. As we were leaving, I saw Ellis Island and the famous immigrant station.

I saw the Statue of Liberty.

The skyline of New York sure was beautiful.

You sure do get good service at meals and in the cabins. There were quite a few passengers on board. We eat our meals in courses with plenty of hands-on service. We'd eat dinner promptly at 7, every night.

All I see during the day is water.
The boat doesn't roll much.

May 20th 1934 Sunday

Aboard the "Paris"

I sure slept sound last night. After breakfast, I walked on deck for about an hour and a ½. I played shuffleboard and deck tennis with Mr. Brown. I got lost looking for my cabin and was late to lunch. Wine is served at the tables. I saw (Jimmy) Durante in a show in the grand salon. After the show, I watched them shoot traps off the side of the boat.

After that, I watched the horseraces.

Mr. Brown gave me some phrases to learn in Spanish and then we walked on the promenade deck. Mr. Brown and I went up to the Grand Salon.

May 21st 1934 Monday

Aboard the "Paris"

It is raining.

I overslept last night. Mr. Brown and I walked on the promenade deck after I got up for the day. We studied Spanish for a while and then I took a nap. Mr. Brown asked me to eat dinner with him and I had to put on my tux.

It's a little longer today.

Mr. Hoover and I saw 2 very funny movies.

I put on my tux in Mr. Brown's room. It was a hard job putting on my collar correctly. It fit alright, but the collar sure did dig into my neck. The whole delegation ate dinner together. The dinner was made special for the delegation. It was very delicious. Our names were embossed on the menu. We had goldware for our dessert course. We went to the Grand Salon to dance. It sure was a swell orchestra. We had a swell midnight lunch. It was all decorated.

May 22nd 1934 Tuesday

Aboard the "Paris"

It is raining and a little rougher, but I do not feel seasick. I went to bed last night at 2 am and got up at 11:20 am. I sure slept well and I had a stroll on deck before lunch. I saw a good movie but it was in French, so I saw another movie.

There was a stage show given by actresses and singers. It was very good.

May 23rd 1934 Wednesday

Aboard the "Paris"

It is a very nice day. I played shuffleboard and deck tennis with Mrs. Mahon. We had tea on deck. Then I played ping pong with Mr. Brown. The orchestra played again at dinner. It was in honor of the captain.

There was a lifeboat drill.

The dinner was very nice.

I saw a movie and I went to bed.

May 24th 1934 Thursday

Aboard the "Paris"

I played shuffleboard with Mr. Brown this morning. I wrote some letters home and watched the races. Mr. Hoover and I went to a movie. The orchestra played at dinner. I wrote letters, watched races, and cleaned my white shoes before going to bed.

May 25th 1934 Friday

Aboard the "Paris"

I got up a little early so I could watch the landing at Plymouth. The coast of England sure was beautiful.

I saw the chalk cliffs.

The countryside was green and very beautiful.

I saw the famous Plymouth lighthouse.

We did not land at a dock but people got on and off from another large boat. The harbor water was very calm as we sailed across it. Havre is a fortified town and quite large.

Little sailboats were sailing around.

The doctor came in a little boat.

There are a lot of gulls following the boat.

We are going through the English Channel and there are a lot of islands. We saw little fisherman's boats darting in between the islands.

I am all packed for disembarking the ship and I wrote my speech. We landed at about 11:30 pm. Mr. and Mrs. Mahon, Mr. Hoover, and I played tennis.

The moonlight was very pretty.

May 26th 1934 Saturday

Havre, France

I got up at 5:30 am and we had a passport and baggage inspection. The Spanish ambassador to France met us at Havre and we are riding first class on the train to Paris.

The countryside is very beautiful.

The boxcars are very small here. The cattle are staked out to graze in the fields. There are thatched roofs on many of the homes and many bicycles.

The trees here are very beautiful.

We saw the famous cathedral in Rouen where Joan of Arc saw her visions.

We traveled along the Seine River.

We arrived in Paris at 10:15am and we went to the Hotel Prince of Wales. I saw the Arc of Triumph. Mr. Hoover, the Pattersons, and I ate lunch in a place which had poor service. Mr. Hoover and I walked around a little. We stopped in a store to buy something where they couldn't speak English. Boy, did we have fun!

The Spanish ambassador came up to see us. I answered the phone to the room when he arrived. It was the first telephone conversation I had in Spanish.

Our suite has eight rooms and it sure is swell!

There is a beautiful patio outside our hotel window.

Francs are bothersome and sure go fast.

The taxis sure do go fast and they have no rules to go by. They just drive. They turn around in the middle of the street. Or anywhere they wish.

The bread here is sold in long round loaves.

There are many beautiful fountains.

Their automobiles sure are small and odd.

May 27th 1934 Sunday

Paris, France

Mr. Brown and I took a long walk around the city.

We went to the Hotel Invalides and there was a moat around it. There are many big guns of many wars there. It is very old and beautiful.

We visited Napoleon's tomb. It was very beautiful as well. There was a dome above it marvelously painted with pictures of Christ. Around the base of the tomb were inlaid the names of victories. There was a very beautiful altar behind the tomb. We also saw other tombs of great Frenchmen such as Joseph Napoleon.

There are many sidewalk cafes and soldiers in Paris. We saw the Italian soldiers that decorated the Arch of Triumph.

We went to the Eiffel Tower and went up. We had to take 3 different elevators. The scene of Paris from that height was very beautiful. It was very high up and the people looked like ants. We could see all of Paris and more. Paris sure is large and extends for a great distance.

The Seine River was very beautiful.

The houses here are really old.

I bought some postcards from up there and I saw a man was cutting silhouettes in half a minute. We then went and ate lunch at a sidewalk café where we met the Pattersons.

The Pattersons and I went through the Louvre. Then we walked through the Luxembourg gardens together.

Coffee costs 3 francs.

Mr. Brown had to pay $1.40 for 2 cigars.

We went through the woods, Boulogne Gardens, and then we had the Spanish ambassador and his wife for dinner that night at the hotel.

May 28th 1934 Monday

Traveling to Spain

We left for Spain.

I saw that many of the houses here have tile roofs and are built right up against the rock.

There was an ox plowing a field. They do not seem to have many tractors.

We paid $1.00 for coffee and rolls and then went through 5 tunnels in succession.

We stopped at Bordeaux and we walked around for about 5 minutes.

Gates are at all roads crossing the railroad.

We saw a great many turpentine trees and also where a great forest fire had burned for miles.

I saw the Bay of Biscay.

The Pyrenees Mountains are very beautiful and high. I've never seen anything like this before.

May 29th 1934 Tuesday

Madrid, Spain

We watched all of the pastoral scenery go by until we reached Spain. The governor of San Sebastian met us at the border. He and his wife were very nice. I spoke Spanish with them. They planned a fiesta for us but we did not arrive soon enough.

We arrived in Madrid about 8am. Representatives met us at the train station and we went to the Palace Hotel. There are a great many beggars in Madrid.

I saw the beautiful post office.

We ate dinner at the Botin Restaurant, which was built in 1622. They say the fire in these ovens has never gone out. We had a good drink called the horchata. I have to use plenty of Spanish to communicate. There are many, many streetcars in Madrid and they all go past the post office and have mailboxes on them. We took a ride in one.

There are no traffic regulations here.

There are plenty of cops, soldiers, and civil guards. The civil guards wear funny hats. They are the crack troops of Spain.

May 30th 1934 Wednesday

Toledo, Spain

Four members of the Spanish congress met us at the train station and went with us. 9 army planes accompanied us as our escort. We had a special coach reserved for us as well.

We saw the very center of Spain on the way.

Two bands met us at the depot.

It was estimated that there were about 25,000 people on the streets.

They took us to the city gate in private cars. It was very old. They took pictures and gave Mr. Hoover the key to the city. They showered us with flowers and rose petals. It was a very beautiful sight as men were dressed in medieval costumes and the girls in mantillas (lace headwraps) and combs.

They took more pictures. Then they took us to the main square. They showered the streets with flowers and the train was decorated with Spanish and American paper and confetti.

The people here were very enthusiastic and showed their emotion very plainly. There were many, many mantillas, shawls, and tapestries hung from the balconies.

We went to the Ayuntamiento (City Hall).

They took even more pictures and I was surrounded only by girls! We had a wonderful lunch. The girls fed me.

We received the army and we then went to the hotel where we had a wonderful dinner.

I sat between two Spanish girls.

The dinner was given by the rotary club.

Mr. C. Bowers, the American ambassador, read the message that President Roosevelt had telephoned. The Governor of San Sebastian was at the dinner when Mr. Hoover spoke.

We went to the palace of Nicaragua and visited his very beautiful flag garden. Then we visited the chapel of the Virgin of the Valley. It was many hundreds of years old. There were underground rooms.

From the garden of the Marques, we saw a turret that had been built in the 17th century. We then visited another chapel and had more to eat. That night we had dinner at 10 o'clock in a beautiful garden. It was very nice. I had a good time with Fernando Segleames and some girls. We returned and went to bed. The Spanish government sent 3 powerful 9-seater cars for us to travel around in. The cars included a chauffeur and footman.

May 31st 1934 Thursday

Toledo, Spain

At 5 o'clock am, there were 3 bands playing outside our window. We viewed the Corpus Christi Procession which was very beautiful. The shrine was made with the first gold brought back from America. The people were dressed very well and many were dressed very oddly.

After the processions, we went to the bullfight and there were 6 bulls and about 6 to 8 horses that were killed. A horse, after being struck by the bull, fell on a man and injured him quite badly. They are very interesting and exciting but the blindfolded horses didn't have a chance.

The bulls came out dashing. It opens with a procession of all the fighters and the like.

The bulls would toss the horses right off the ground. The people threw their hats at the bull when a fighter was in danger and I saw another horse fall on a man. One of the matadors was only 19.

The fight opens with bandilleros who tease and stick darts in the bull. The picadors are the ones who ride horses and spear the bull. After the picadors, the matador kills the bull with a sword which he runs between the bull's front shoulder blades. He first performs with the bulls a little. The sword goes into the bull up to the hilt. Three decorated mules drag the bull out. The matador walks around the ring. The bullfighters are dressed very picturesquely.

That evening, we visited the cigarral of St. Soldevilla where we had dinner. I met some nice senoritas. It was a very beautiful garden. We did not go to bed until 3 am.

June 1st 1934 Friday

Toledo, Spain

In the morning, we visited the Alcazar of Charles V. The Alcazar is a military academy and it was built on a battle site.

During our visit, we saw exhibitions of skills given by cadets. We also visited the central military gymnastic school and saw their classrooms of war where they study guns, gas mask development, etc.

The students gave a demonstration of gymnastics. They threw a bar which would correspond with our javelin but much heavier. It is the Bask bar. They had a lavish lunch prepared for us. We have lunch after every place we visit, and that is many. The many meals are very good, though.

Tonight we dressed in our tuxes and went to the theatre where they are going to present the gold medal to Toledo. It was broadcasted. There were speeches by both mayors, the U.A. ambassadors, and others. The delegation received medals from the government. In fact, I did not because I was too young. We arrived at the hotel again at a late hour. There was a show afterward by dancers.

June 2nd 1934 Saturday

Toledo, Spain

They named a street in honor of Toledo, Ohio. There were speeches given and moving pictures taken of it. There was an official dinner given at the hotel for the U.A. ambassador and Toledo delegation. We ate again. We visited the cathedral and saw the most famous painting of El Greco. The cathedral was very beautiful and old. There were many carved figures. The rafters were even carved. We saw them working in gold gilding. They make the design without a traced figure to follow.

We visited another old cathedral with more old hand carvings. We went to the cigarral of Dr. Maranon. He is a great man of Spain. He is a famous doctor, writer, and politician. His daughter and son were very nice. We had lunch again. I sure like orchestras. His home is very beautiful. There is a little chapel in it with a beautiful altar. We saw his wine cellar which contained many, many bottles of wine. Some of it a century old.

While we were there, the Count of Romanones came. He is also another famous man of Spain. He was prime minister about 10 times.

Dr. Maranon and the count and another man got together and told the king that he had to leave.

Tonight we went to a theater and saw part of a very good play. We then went to the bullring where there was a dance held in our honor. Mr. Brown and Mr. Hoover received a bouquet of flowers just as the women did. There was a large crowd.

After the broadcast, we went to a beautiful garden and had a party. It was very nice and I met some very nice girls. We didn't get home until very late.

June 3rd 1934 Sunday

Toledo, Spain

We went to the cathedral for church this morning. The altar was certainly very pretty. They presented us with a piece of stone from the cathedral. They showed us all around. It certainly was large. We saw many marvelous paintings, old jewels, and ancient costumes. We saw a robe with 70,000 jewels of unknown value. There were also beautiful, large, gold and silver plates, and many other things of beauty. Everything dates back for centuries.

We went to the postimal school. Mr. Hoover, after a few speeches, went up and said something to the head of the school. He told me that he had said, 'Don't you think you ought to hear from the student?' So I gave the speech that I had written on the ship. I was not the least bit nervous and I had to stand in a pulpit on a box. I think I gave it quite well, for there was a great deal of applause. After I had taken my seat, I had to get back up so that they would quit applauding. The Toledo delegation was quite proud of me.

Mr. Brown was not there for all day because he was sick with indigestion. He had fainted when he got out of bed this morning. I was not nervous after I finished. I talked about the correspondence between the 2 Toledos and used a spark and flame as an illustration.

The school children sang songs. They sang very well. At the beginning of their singing, they let loose many pigeons and it made a very pretty sight. After the end of the program, everyone congratulated me and the students carried me out on their shoulders. I shook hands with just about everybody in town.

I had my picture taken and had about 75–100 students carry me about the city shouting "Viva el estudiante". They then took me to the hotel where I then had to give them my address and name.

Today, we went to a typical festival organized by "Pena Villata". It was the playing of bands, horsemanship, and bullfighting. The horseman jumped over humans and other hurdles. Masked men chased each other for a rose. It was very interesting and wonderful horsemanship. Bullfighting followed. We stayed for one bull. This bullfight consisted of very small bulls and inexperienced bullfighters.

I did not like this at all. The bull did not have a chance because it was so small. It didn't know what to do and he fell all over himself. He knocked down the matador 2 or 3 times and the matador would try to push him away. After he killed him, the matador cut off his ear as a trophy.

We left as we had to meet with the count of Romanones at home. It certainly was marvelous. We ate again. I didn't do much because I was too dead-tired. When we got back to the hotel, I went to bed at about 8. I got up and dressed at 10:30 to go to another party but I got sick and vomited. I did not go to the party and stayed in bed.

June 4th Monday

Toledo, Spain

After I got up and dressed, I went down to the lobby as we were going to a ball. About 8 students met me and wanted to take me out about the town. The delegation went to the ball where we received a great welcome. I danced 3 dances and quit because they danced too slow. The boys and I walked about the town. We had to speak all Spanish.

We found a newborn puppy and it was very small. It was near the wall where we were looking out at the Tajo River. We went through many winding streets and returned to the ball. The street had grooves on both sides of the wall so that cars could pass through.

We visited a ceramic shop where we saw beautiful tile work. It belongs to the girl with whom Bill corresponds with. She gave me something, I think an ashtray, which she sent to the hotel.

We visited an art school where we saw marvelous work by the students. I received a beautiful plate. We went to the national factory of arms. They were making plenty of ammunition. They presented a beautiful sword to Toledo, Ohio. We saw them test the army swords by bending, striking, and cutting steel with them. They presented us with razor blades, a razor case, and a pair of gold ornamented scissors. We saw the workers making razor blades, shells for big guns and cartridges. We had another little lunch.

We then went to the Castarias which is the Palace of Count of Fircat. It was quite a distance away. In his home, there were old armoire chairs dating back for centuries. We also saw a carrying carriage. We had another enormous dinner. I saw the signatures of Ferdinand and Isabel. We saw the law books of the Indies and many other valuable old books. The count had 10,000 acres. It is also on a mountain where they have wild boar and deer. We went back and saw a very old monastery. We have guards that carry rifles to protect the property.

The Aqueduct that carries water to his house is 400 years old. It is made of stone. We walked about and saw a wonderful view of the countryside from the hill and then returned. There is plenty of snow on the mountaintops.

I returned in the open car which went 70 mph. We saw mules as a power supply pumping water for irrigation, I went to bed and I got up to get dressed to go to a ball. I was sick and vomited. I stayed in bed.

June 5th 1934 Tuesday

Toledo, Spain

I feel good today.

We went to a nearby small town called Talaveras (Talaver de la Reina) where we received a great reception and had a large dinner. We then went to the home of the owner of a ceramics factory. We saw them working with tiles and clay. It was very interesting. They certainly are great artists. I received a clay inkstand.

We then went to the town hall where we had a large dinner. We then went to another small town called Oropesa. Here, the women and men dress in a typical provincial dress. It is very colorful and beautiful. They presented a mock-wedding for us in order to see the colorful array.

Both man and woman put a ring on each other. They said something to some coins and presented them to the people. A robe was thrown over both their shoulders. They then went to the town square with everybody and there was a dance. They used lemons with coins stuck in them. Even a very small boy danced. This couple had been married 15 days before.

The women in this town are not good-looking. Even small girls look very old in the face. We went to a home. They shared one of their beds with us. It was very high. It had 3 mattresses, many colorful covers, and a roof like an old colonial bed. The rest of the home was very beautiful. The dishes in the kitchen were hanging on the walls. We saw some babies which they said were only a few months old. And even they had on a picturesque dress.

We then went to Lagartera. It was also very picturesque. We went to an old castle. I went up one of the towers. The stairs were very small, stone, and winding. It was very dark. The top was small and was typical of places from where they fight. The scenery from there was very beautiful with plains stretching afar with high mountains as a background. They are harvesting here and they cut everything with a sickle or scythe. We had another lunch and returned to Toledo.

June 6th 1934 Wednesday

Toledo, Spain

In the morning, we packed the gifts in the trunks. I received a small handmade paper opener. I lost my comb and after getting up, I had to put on my hat as my hair was uncombed. I needed a haircut and went and got one.

We left at 3 in one of the big cars for Madrid. We went 110 kilometers an hour! We went so fast that we had to stop in order to let gas flow into the carburetor. They sure are good drivers. At night, we went to the embassy of U.A. in honor of the commissions of both Toledos! It was a farewell party. It was very nice. I sure hated to say goodbye because I had made such good friends. There were tears in many eyes.

After the party, we returned to the hotel. It was a very nice garden that the ambassador had. At 10:30, Mr. Perezagua, Mr. Hoover, Mr. Brown, Perezagua's brother, and I went to the theater. Afterward, we went to eat dinner which was at 2am. Mrs. Patterson was presented a medal at the party.

June 7th 1934 Thursday

Madrid, Spain

I didn't get up until late. Mr. Brown, Mr. Hoover, and I went to the theater to see the newsreel about us. I saw myself in the movies. The reel was very nice and there were more people on the streets to receive us than I had thought. Perezagua came and said goodbye to us before he returned to Toledo. He and Mr. Hoover were almost in tears.

Tonight, while Mr. Brown and I were sitting at a sidewalk café, we saw an automobile accident. A man was injured.

June 8th 1934 Friday

Madrid, Spain

I put on my scout uniform. Everybody sure looked at me funny. They must have thought I was a socialist with my red neckerchief. It was quite warm with those leggings and heavy stockings.

We saw a man driving a flock of goats through the middle of town.

They are having a lot of socialist troubles and there are cops everywhere. We went to the embassy and saw Mr. and Mrs. Bowers. Mr. Bowers showed us a carriage that a count had used. It was the same kind the king used and it sure was beautiful with all of the ornamentation.

Everybody is talking about the celebration of the 2 Toledos! It has raised quite a stir in regards to such close friendship.

June 9th 1934 Saturday

Madrid, Spain

We found a very good German restaurant to eat in. It is called The Heidelberg. I saw the greatest bullfighter of Spain. His name is "El Gaya". We saw Perezagua again today. This afternoon we went with Mrs. Patterson who laid a very large wreath on the monument of the woman who made it possible for women to go to the university. We got on a train for Sevilla at 10:40 pm and we rode all night and slept in our compartment.

June 10th 1934 Sunday

Sevilla, Spain

We arrived here at 9am. Mr. Brown and I went to the Hotel Paris because it was cheaper. It is horribly hot here. There are a great many hacks here instead of taxis. We went and saw a little of the cathedral. It is very large.

When you go out, there is a large line of beggars to meet you at the door.

This afternoon, we went on a sightseeing tour. We went to the Alcazar first. It is an old palace with much tile work and carving. The king used to come to live here. The household fixtures and furnishings are still there. There were many tapestries but they had been taken down when Spain became a republic. It dates back to the 16th century when it was remodeled by Charles IV. The tile work is very beautiful. The carpets date back many hundreds of years. The palace gardens are very beautiful. It covers 40 acres. Pine trees are trimmed in arches. The magnolia blossoms are very beautiful and big. We then visited some very old patios.

We went to the home of the Duke of Alba. His garden was very pretty. We saw tangerines growing. The duke used to have different colored horses and a differently dressed driver every day when he rode in his coaches.

We saw remains of the Roman walls which were built in the 10th century. We went through Maria Luisa Park, which was very beautiful. We saw the exposition building of the countries when the world's fair was in Sevilla. While sitting on our balcony watching the people in the plaza, I saw lamplighters lighting the street lamps. We walked about and went to bed early.

June 11th 1934 Monday

Sevilla, Spain

At 4:30 am, a cart went by and Mr. Brown and I both woke up thinking that somebody (Mr. Hoover) was knocking on our door. We met the Mahons who had arrived last night from Granada. We walked about and did some shopping. The main street does not have any vehicle traffic but plenty of beggars.

At 2:40 pm, the Pattersons and Mr. Hoover left on the train for Granada. It sure is hot here. All of the shops close from 1pm to 5pm. We walked around the park and returned to the hotel to take a siesta. The Mahons came to our hotel. The Mahons, Mr. Brown, and I ate dinner together and took a walk and had coffee at a café. We stopped and looked in many store windows. We retired early for dinner. We had 2 kinds of fish and two kinds of meat to eat.

June 12th 1934 Tuesday

Sevilla, Spain

Before going out, I tried to fix a roll of film in my camera but couldn't do it right. Neither could Mr. Brown. We went to a camera shop where I had another roll put in. I had ruined the one I monkeyed with.

We went to the cathedral where we saw the tomb of Columbus. The 4 figures holding the tomb represent the 4 kingdoms of Navarre, Leon, Castile, and Aragon. We saw San Antonio de Padua. It is one of the most famous paintings of Murillo. The figure of San Antonio was cut out by a thief and it turned up in the home of J.P. Morgan. It has been restored. We saw the lines of cutting.

We also saw some famous paintings of Goya. We then climbed the Giralda Tower. It is very old and was a mosque built by the moors. There were no steps up; it had inclined walks like a gangplank. It was a very interesting view from the top. Mr. Brown and I walked about town and got lost. We saw the market. Our walk was very interesting.

Mrs. Mahon, Mr. Brown, and I went shopping after our siestas. It was very hot. The rest went for a ride in a carriage but I did not go because I wanted to go shopping at a certain store and they were going to leave right away and we wouldn't get back in time as the store closed at 8.

The maid brought back the shirts I had sent to get washed but they were not ironed. She said she didn't have enough time to do it. The Mahons left on the 10:10pm train for Madrid on their way to Paris.

June 13th 1934 Wednesday

Sevilla, on our way to Algeciras

We got up at 5:45 and ate breakfast. We met an American woman and her daughter who were going on the same bus as us to Algeciras. We went on a bus because it took 12 hours by train and only 5 hours by bus. Also, we did not want to use all of our kilometra tickets as the bus is cheaper.

It started out like a shot. At the same time, another company started and there was a race between the two almost all the way to Algeciras. It was very interesting on the way. We saw the peasants' homes real close and saw the people working. The other bus stopped and we passed them. Going along all the time with this fantastic race, I had a feeling we would have an accident, and we did! I even thought about how I would splint broken bones and how I would duck down.

I was sitting in the seat next to the aisle. I was dozing off when I suddenly looked up and saw a car almost in the middle of the road. It had come out of a drive. The bus driver jerked on the wheel in order to miss him. He then had to jerk again the other way in order not to go off the road and he had to turn again the other way and I thought everything would be OK but he turned the other way and I was thrown on top of Mr. Brown.

I could feel the bus tipping. The bus turned over completely so that the wheels were sticking straight up in the air. It happened very quickly. When the bus stopped moving, I found myself in Mr. Brown's seat by an open window. I crawled out right away so that I could help the others out.

I helped out two men and a woman. It was the American lady that we had met at breakfast. I was afraid that it might start a fire as gasoline was spread over everything. The two Spanish men who got out of the bus quite quickly embraced and kissed each other.

I did not suffer the least bump or the slightest scratch. Mr. Brown cut his hands breaking a window so he could get out. He was thrown on the opposite side of the coach. He also got bruises on the hip, elbow, and chin. The bus fell first on our side. The lady I helped out did not want to get out right away but laid on the ground and groaned. The driver of the car was pulling his hair.

A girl was out behind the car.

A man was cut slightly on the forehead.

A Frenchman was scratched on his bald head.

An American was injured the worst. He hurt his arm, shoulder, side, and leg but nothing was wounded or broken. The American lady hurt her ankle but her daughter was uninjured. The bus driver was not hurt but his assistant cut his arm. I guess I suffered the least of them all.

A man who lived nearby saw it all and he said that he thought not one of us would get out alive. Our baggage was all smashed. My suitcase had a hole knocked through it and the corners were wrecked. One end was knocked out of Mr. Brown's. Many bags were completely ruined. They think it was the bags on the roof that prevented the bus from turning over again. If the bags had been on the inside and the windows closed, it would have been a different story.

The Spaniard who saw it was very kind. He invited us into his house to eat and rest until another bus came. We had some milk and cookies at the man's house.

Baggage was strewn all over. I got my hat out of the street about ten feet from the bus. One lady's pocketbook was under the bus between the street and roof of the bus.

The injured girl was taken to the hospital. We were taken to the nearest town in a bus that came after us: the bus we had been racing came after us, stopped to help us if need be, and then went on.

After traveling awhile, we stopped at a place to get a drink and something to eat. In this other bus, the injured girl's mother, who weighed about 400 pounds, sat directly behind a different driver and kept a check on him for many long hours.

We saw many cattle and goats in the plains that stretched between the high mountains. We saw some cork trees. They looked funny with part of their bark taken off. We saw them making charcoal.

We passed many trains of donkeys and burros loaded with charcoal, grains and wood, etc. One time, the bus had to stop to pick up a package of newspapers that had blown off.

We saw them threshing by driving horses round and round over the crops that had been on a clear and smooth spot of ground. After it was trampled, they threw it up into the air and the wind carried away the chaff and left the grain.

We arrived an hour and a half late. We went to our hotel and cleaned up. We went to the Pattersons and Mr. Hoover's hotel but they had gone to Gibraltar.

We tried to have our bags replaced but they didn't do anything about it. This evening, the American, Frenchman, Mr. Brown, and I went to the fair. There were many things we paid to see. We saw a woman ride a motorcycle around a circular wall, which was about 20 feet high and perpendicular to the ground. She sure was good. She would go around so fast that her body would be straight out from the wall. She would come up to the top of the wall. She would go around without her hands on the steering wheel and once, she took off her jacket while going around. She would even zig-zag. It was too dangerous for the little money that she made.

While we had been traveling in the bus, we had gone past Cadiz and traveled along the Mediterranean. We saw them making salt by allowing pools of seawater to evaporate. The sea breeze was wonderful.

We also went through the southernmost point of Europe. It is called Tarifa. We could see the mountains of

Africa on the other side of the Mediterranean. The water in the Mediterranean was very blue. After the fair, we saw the rock of Gibraltar. It was very big and at night was very pretty with lights on it which sparkled in the water.

June 14th 1934 Thursday

Algeciras, Spain

It was plenty noisy outside our window this morning.

We tried to get something out of the bus company for another suitcase but accomplished nothing. The Pattersons, Mr. Hoover, and Mr. Mahon went to Africa on the 3pm boat. I didn't go because it would cost about 5 dollars and they would only be there for a couple of hours, and besides, Mr. Brown and I were going over later anyways.

While they were gone, I took a bath, repacked my wrecked suitcase, and studied Spanish. I met them at the boat after dinner. Mr. Brown and I took a walk and then went to bed early.

June 15th 1934 Friday

Algeciras, Spain

This morning, when I got up and sat on the bed to dress, I noticed my handkerchief on the chair and I was sure that I had not put it there. Then I noticed that my traveler's checks were on top of my suitcase. I knew that there had been a thief because my pants were bunched up and my passport card and kilometra tickets were spread on the suitcase and out of my coat pocket.

My wallet was gone.

15 pesetas and my pearl-handled knife was gone from my pocket where I had kept my traveler's checks. I had by this time told Mr. Brown and he too noticed his pants, traveler's checks, railroad tickets, and passport on the floor. They took 25 pesetas from him. He had a hundred in his wallet and he had taken that to bed with him.

We went out to the balcony to see how the thief had gotten in. We were on the second floor. We could see where his feet had rubbed against the wall as he climbed up a pipe. When I got out on the balcony, I found my wallet with everything out of it spread out on the floor. Later, we found that our pens were missing.

I lost a knife, 15 pesetas, my Ever Sharpe, and my fountain pen. Mr. Brown lost his fountain pen and 25 pesetas. We were however lucky as the thief could have taken passports, our railroad tickets, and traveler's checks, which would have cost a lot of trouble.

The Pattersons and Mr. Hoover sailed today from Gibraltar so Mr. Brown and I went over with them on the 3pm boat to see them off; they did not sail until about 9pm. Meanwhile, we ate, stopped at a café, and did some shopping. Things were very cheap.

We saw English "bobbies" (cops). The Rock of Gibraltar is enormous.

Mr. Brown and I had to leave before they sailed as the last boat for Algeciras left at 7pm. They saw us off. We had to go through customs. They searched others very closely but just pushed us through without even looking at us.

We saw the "Rex" pull into Gibraltar's harbor. It certainly was a big boat. It looked like a small town, all lit up. We went to bed early as we had to get up early to go to Africa.

June 16th 1934 Saturday

Algeciras to Africa

We got up at six and had to get our passports checked. The boat was to leave at 7 but did not because there was too much fog across the straits. We rode 3rd class. It was very interesting. We saw very large fish jumping out of the water and I saw 9 French and Spanish battleships anchored in a straight line at Gibraltar. We could see Gibraltar in the distance all the way across the coasts which were a very dazzling white. All homes and buildings are whitewashed. After landing, we went and had our passports fixed so we could go to Tetuan.

We brought no baggage with us and we had worn dark shirts and brought our toothbrushes. We saw many Moorish women. They were veiled and dressed in white. The men wore turbans or red hats. They wore large garments and no socks but shoes that I don't see how they kept on. There were many Moors on the bus to Tetuan.

On the way, we had to stop at a small place for customs and have our passports okayed. It was much like a desert. The journey was very interesting. The Moors sure wear plenty of clothes. When we arrived, we went to Hotel

Repicua. We took a walk through a little part of the Moorish district. A small Moor served as our guide.

The shops are about 8–10 feet square. The people put their wares right on the street and sell them. The small children have all their hair cut off except a spot about 3 inches in diameter that is braided into a long pigtail. The unmarried men wear turbans that cover all but a part of their head. I took some interesting pictures. The men smoke long pipes. Their shoes are very clumsy. Their feet are very thick with calluses.

In the meat market, the meat hangs right out in the open with no refrigeration. We saw the public letter writer and gave money-changes. The women who clean the streets wear very large hats. They go barefoot most of the time and wear leggings. The Moors drink a great deal of peppermint tea. The men have long beards and wear long robes. The homes are way back on the side streets with hardly any light. Their doors are very large and they get jammed together when they go to the water fountain. Men do their business of buying and selling right in the middle of the streets.

The streets have no sidewalks and are about 10 to 12 feet wide. Horses and buses are always going up and down the streets. We went to the part where they were washing, drying, tanning, and cleaning skins (goats, cow, and sheep). We saw a Moorish cemetery.

We returned to the hotel, ate, and took a siesta. We took another walk with the same boy. We saw the same things again and went to a museum. There we saw a lot of Moorish guns, saddles, sabers, clothes, and their dining rooms. There are no tables or chairs in it but a low couch where they lay and eat. We also saw the kitchen implements and the chair that they carried the bride in to her husband.

After leaving, a man met us and said he was going to have the Moor boy arrested because it was unlawful for a boy without a license to do this. He called a cop and they took him away. There was a big argument. They took him to the jail where he had to sign his name and they let him go. We had to find our own way back to the hotel but we found it alright.

After dinner, we walked some more and went to a café that had an orchestra. I was sure glad to get into bed.

June 17th 1934 Sunday

Tetuan, Morocco

We took a walk this morning through the Moorish part of the city, but without our guide. We did some shopping. I bought 2 pairs of slippers, 3 wallets, and a red hat. We saw the same things as yesterday. We watched a boy judge bread and put it in different classes as it was taken from the oven. The ovens are right in the street but down under the ground.

There was an argument between a woman and a boy about some article. They both were crying their heads off. The money-changers are right on the street. We also went through the Jewish district. We went through the fish market and none of the fish were packed in ice and didn't have any type of refrigeration.

This afternoon, we all went to the "La Playa" (beach) and walked around watching them swim. We returned in a dumpy bus. We saw two African soldiers arrest a man. We walked around after dinner and went to bed.

June 18th 1934 Monday

Tetuan to Xaver

Everybody knows about the fight between (Max) Baer and Carnera, even here in Africa.

We left on the 9am bus. The bus was very old and about ready to fall apart. The trip was very interesting and the turns were very sharp. We were going uphill most of the time. We saw them building a new road. They put large rocks to make the road and then broke them up right in the road. We passed a large army camp on the way. The houses were grouped around in a circle. There were also a lot of tents. Machine guns were set up.

After arriving in Xaver, we went to the hotel. After eating lunch, we went to the proprietors and asked him if he would cash some traveler's checks for us so we would have some money. There is no bank in Xaver. He wouldn't do it and said he had never seen any before.

Moorish waiters served our meals. The proprietor, through a great deal of courtesy, said we could stay overnight as otherwise, we would have had to return to Tetuan. He said we could send him the money later. He even offered to loan us some money to use in Xaver.

The market is in front of the hotel. On the one side, the straight and high walls of the mountains ascend. The whole town is surrounded by high mountains. You can hear the rushing of water from the mountains.

Late in the afternoon, we took a walk with a Moorish boy as a guide. He too trusted us for the money we would have to pay him. He took us first to the Alcazar, which was an old Moorish fort. On top of its turrets were some stork nests. Inside of its ancient walls was a beautiful garden. They had some monkeys that they had caught in the mountains in cages.

In the Alcazar, he showed us the dungeons. They were very dark and we could see the chains that they used. We went to a school where they made carpets. Children from about 6 years old and up did the work. It was very interesting to watch them as they did the work very well.

When the carpet has been completed, a pair of shears is used to shear the top of the rug smooth. We asked the price of a 14x15 rug; it would cost about $60. We then walked through the small cobblestoned and narrow street to see the small shops.

We saw a girl without a nose.

We visited the jail. There were about 9 prisoners. There were many money changers everywhere. When two Moors greet each other, they kiss each other's hand and then their own.

We walked to the mountain and saw the water come gushing out from the sides. Women were washing clothes on the rocks. The water was troughed off in different directions. One place, there was such a velocity of water that it was flowing uphill. We followed one of these troughs and saw two flour mills. They were very small in size and water served as the power to turn the large stone disc that crushed the grain. The rocks served as scrubbing-boards for the women to wash.

We returned to the hotel; there was a large crowd in a circle. In the middle, there were two men. One was talking in Moorish and beating a pair of large shears at the same time, and the other man was dancing. The Moors were greatly amused and it was very interesting. We did not take a walk after dinner because there were no streetlights.

Before we returned, we saw the Moors entering a mosque. They take their shoes off before entering.

Xaver is a town with a population of about 7,000 Moors, 200 Jews, and 80 Spaniards. In 1920, the town was occupied for the first time in its history by any foreigners. It was the Spanish under General Berenguer.

June 19th 1934 Tuesday

Xaver to Tetuan to Ceuta to Algeciras

We traveled all day in buses. We got up at 6am. The bus from Xaver to Tetuan was very poor. We had to stop every once in a while to get water. We had to wait about 2 hours in Tetuan before getting another bus to Ceuta. This bus was a very good one and we got to Ceuta very quickly. In Ceuta, we had to wait 5 hours before catching our boat to Algeciras.

The trip to Algeciras was very interesting. We watched them load cars on the boat. On the way over, we saw many large fish jump about 5 feet out of the water. At Algeciras, we had to go through customs but did not have to pay anything. We went to the hotel and we sure were glad to get our African clothes off as we had not taken any baggage with us. After dinner, we walked about and went to bed early.

June 20th 1934 Wednesday

Algeciras to Malaga

After getting up, we washed up real good and took a walk. We went to the bus company to see about our claims but nothing had been done. At 12:45, we got on our train for Malaga. It was very hot. We stopped every 10 minutes at the same type of railroad station, where many people were selling refreshments.

The scenery was very beautiful. I saw the second reaper that I had seen in Spain. He cut the crop with sickles. The olive groves were certainly kept in good condition. At every small path or road, there was a guard chain across the road. We stopped at Bobadilla for 40 minutes and had to change trains.

We passed through a small town called El Chorro. Nearby there is a large gorge which is very deep and very beautiful.

The train passed through one tunnel after another.

When we arrived at Malaga, we went to the hotel and took a walk afterward. There was a lot of police in Malaga as they had been having trouble.

June 21st 1934 Thursday

Malaga, Spain

In the morning, we went to the beach. There were quite a few bathers. For the rest of the day, we did nothing but walk around and sit in cafes. We walked through a very beautiful park. At the beach, we saw a very interesting aquarium.

June 22nd 1934 Friday

Malaga, Spain

This morning, we went to Torremolinos in a small bus. It is a quaint little fishing town. We caught the train and went to El Chorro, which is another small town in this province. We sent our bags on to Gobantes. When we left El Chorro, we walked to Gobantes. It was about 8 miles in distance. We carried a lunch with us which was made in Malaga. The walk was exceedingly beautiful. We did quite a bit of climbing. A walk was built out perpendicular from the wall of the gorge.

We walked along this and every once in a while, we would see the river that ran underground through the mountains. The gorge was very deep and very pretty where the river had worn large grooves in the sides of the gorge. There were very large rocks in the river. During our walk, we had to go through several long tunnels where we could hardly see our way through. There were several waterfalls and it made a very pretty scene with large hawks soaring above and fish swimming lazily in the blue water below.

The sides of the gorge were certainly high and steep. The path was about 3 feet wide and at some places only about 2! On the other side of the gorge, we could see the tunnels of the railroad trains. We passed a few large dams that held back great quantities of water.

The river behind the dams was very large. We were lost several times and lost much time and energy. We went through one tunnel which was so long that we were not able to see in it but just had to walk.

When we did arrive at Gobantes, we almost did not get a place to stay overnight as there was no hotel there and the very small inn that was there did not have any vacant beds, but the proprietor said we could stay in the beds of the men who would not be there that night. We had to take that, or sleep in the mountains.

The room had 4 beds. Before retiring for the night, we sat downstairs. We saw working men all eating out of the same dish. They sure ate plenty! They had told us that there would be no one else in the room but when we started to get in bed, another man came in. I wore both my underwear and pajamas. This other fellow lit a match and looked real close at his bed then put a jacket in between his covers. I didn't sleep very well and this other fellow was always waking up, lighting matches and looking at his bed.

He ran into bedbugs. He talked to himself a lot.

June 23rd 1934 Saturday

Gobantes to Granada

Our bill for all the gracious beds and breakfast was only 4 pesetas a piece. We got a 12am train for Bobadilla, third-class. Third class sure is interesting. We changed trains at Bobadilla and rode first-class to Granada. It was a very pretty ride and at every station, we got off the train and stood around until it started again. We got to Granada at 5:30.

We were very dirty so we took a bath. While walking around, I saw a mule fall over from exhaustion and they about pulled its tail out, getting it up. It would get up and fall right over again.

We walked around and sat at a café. When leaving the café, we saw streetcars hit each other as one had gone off the track, but no one was injured. We went to bed early considering their hours.

June 24th 1934 Sunday

Granada, Spain

We went to visit Alhambra today. We had to go in a cogwheel streetcar to get up the hill to it. The rose gardens were very beautiful. The architecture alone was wonderful. It must have taken years to build it as the rock was all hand-carved, which was a great deal of carving. Some of the rock had holes carved right through it.

We saw the large beautiful open pool where the sultan's wives bathed. There was a wonderful view from it. The court of the lions was very beautiful with a fountain sprinkling down and water coming out of their mouths. They do not look much like lions. The religion of the Moors does not allow them to paint or carve living figurines.

We saw the ambassador's room where the men held their official meetings. It was a very beautiful room. We saw the bathtub of the princess and of others also.

There was a room where the Sultans had all their heads cut off.

We went to the princess' palace. It was one of the large towers. It showed where her bedroom was located and other notable rooms. We climbed several of the towers and got a wonderful view of the city. We climbed the largest watchtower which was El Torre Novella.

We visited the palace of Charles V which was large and massive but not as beautiful as the Alhambra. It is very close to Alhambra though. I bought some handmade lace on the sides of the Alhambra walls. We returned to the hotel, ate, and had a siesta.

After our siesta, we walked about and then went to the cathedral where we saw the tomb of Ferdinand and Isabel, Juana La Loca (her husband), and Felipe el Hermioso (who was a prince from the Austrian Hapsburg line). They were under the floor before the altar. They were very crude and clumsy looking. Ferdinand and Isabel were side by side on a table in the center and the others on the sides of the rooms. We then went around the cathedral and saw paintings and other things of interest.

We saw the flags of the campaigns against the Moors. We saw embroidery work done by Isabel and some old coins. We returned to our hotel and then went to the gypsy quarters. There we saw the gypsies who dress and keep their old customs to amuse tourists in order to make a living. Some small girls danced for us and we gave them some coppers. We were mobbed by them as they were begging for money and cigarettes. In one place, we stood in the doorway and watched them dance. We wanted to enter and they wanted to charge us 50 pesetas, so we stayed out.

One old woman showed us her home for a few coppers. It was built right into the mountain. The rooms were carved out of stone and had a round roof of rock. The dishes hung right on the walls. While waiting for the bus to return, a man very kindly asked us to sit down in front of his home until the bus came. After dinner, we walked Gran Via and went to bed early. Saw considerable works of Alonso Cano.

June 25th 1934 Monday

Granada to Madrid

We left on the 8:25am train to Moredas. We rode third-class and took our lunch with us, as the trains don't carry diners. We were going to ride 3rd class only to Moredas, but the people were so nice we rode 3rd class all the way to Madrid. Another reason is that we wanted to save on kilometra tickets until later.

The train was crowded as many were going to Madrid for the canonization of a Savior. The third-class seats were hard wood and had very straight backs. At Moreda, we changed trains, with the same people in our compartment. It was very hot, but the Spaniards suffered more than we did.

Everybody had brought their own lunch. We ate on the trains. We had tortillas, ham, bread, breaded pork chops, and fruit. We changed trains again at Baena. The countryside was very pretty, with men harvesting and threshing. Some of the smaller mountains were very pretty and were covered with olive trees. One woman in our compartment was sure funny, especially the way she slept with her eyes half open.

From Baena to Madrid, we had better seats. They were leather. We arrived in Madrid at 8:20pm, all tired and dirty after 12 hours on the train. We washed, ate, and had our first glass of water since we left Madrid 16 days ago. We walked over to the palace hotel to see if we had any mail. We returned, washed our soot-laden hair, and went to bed.

June 26th 1934 Tuesday

Madrid, Spain

This morning, I went to the palace hotel and got a badly needed haircut and our suitcases; Mr. Brown went to the American counsel for our mail. We were sure glad to get some mail. We had also gone to the post office but there was nothing there.

Mr. Brown cashed a traveler's check and it took 35 minutes to do it. We walked around and sat in cafes. After dinner, we walked over to the palace hotel again. We went to bed at 11:30, which is early for the Spaniards.

June 27th 1934 Wednesday

Madrid, Spain

We got up early and went out and bought a badly needed pen. We wrote until 9:30. The banks opened at 9:30. It took Mr. Brown 1 hour and 40 minutes to cash our government check and convert it to traveler's checks. We took our passports to the police station. After dinner, we wrote cards for about 2 hours. We had also bought another pen before lunch. We got our palace hotel bill, which was 920 pesetas for the 7 of us for 6 days. We returned to the hotel.

I caught up in my diary. It felt good to write with a fountain pen again. We expected some mail from Toledo to be brought by a friend. Mr. Salino had coffee with us in a café. He was the man who was to bring us our mail but he only brought some for Mr. Brown.

June 28th 1934 Thursday

Madrid, Spain

We got up early this morning as we had a lot to do. It seems funny not to be going to catch trains and having 3 men and a horse take us and 2 suitcases to the depot. I was going on Cook's tour but I couldn't as they were needed and Mr. Brown had too much to do. I hunted for scout headquarters and walked a lot doing it. When I did get there, I found out that they had moved 4 months ago.

This afternoon, I took a real bath during siesta. We went to the America Insurance Company to see about the bus accident but they were closed. Then we went to the ABC office to get copies of the paper with pictures and articles of the Toledo S Delegation (2 Toledos). Then we headed for the newspaper offices of the Grafico and Cueta el Mundial to get more pictures but on the way, we passed the place where Mr. Brown had lived 10 years ago. He had been looking very hard for the family he had lived with. He went in and asked a grocer, who gave him some encouraging news.

From there, we went to the police station to get our passports. They searched us before we could enter. We walked around for 4 hours this afternoon doing these things. I got another letter from home today.

Mr. Brown had made connections with the family he lived with 10 years ago. Mr. Galino ate dinner with us tonight and afterward, we went to the beach. The beach was a very wonderful one for being artificial.

The river was dammed to furnish the water and sand was hauled in to give the appearance. It was very wonderful as it had cafes, roller skating, etc. We went to see a game of fronton Jai Alai today. The fronton games are very interesting. The game is something like handball and played on a much larger court and is much harder and swifter. Girls played tonight. The ball is made out of a composition of goatskin. It is about as big and hard as a golf ball but it doesn't bounce as easy. They use paddles, tennis rackets, and sometimes their hands. We went home around 1:30am and they still had not finished.

June 29th 1934 Friday

Madrid, Spain

This morning, I went to the newspaper offices of The Cronica and Mundo Grafico to get more papers. This afternoon we walked around the El Parque del Buen Retiro (the central park of Madrid). It was very large and beautiful. There was a small body of water in which boats were rowed around. At the water's edge, there was a large and beautiful statue of Alfonso XII.

From there, we rode the metro (subway) to the bullring. There was no fighting today but we just went to the ring. Mr. Brown found out where the family he lived with 10 years ago resided. So, after dinner, he went there and I went to the theatre in town which was called the "Capitol" and I saw a very good show. I went at 10:30 and got back at 12:30. At 1:30, Mr. Brown and Ernestro, who was the son of the woman where he lived, came in. He invited us to go to the bullfight on Sunday.

June 30th 1934 Saturday

Madrid, Spain

I went to the American Consulate this morning to get mail. There was nothing for me, but Mr. Brown received some things. Mr. Brown and I had some pastry, which we had for Dad's birthday celebration in Spain. We received all the copies of the ABC today and it made up quite a bundle. We had an appointment with a man at 2:30 at a Café Molinero but he didn't show up.

Tonight, I ate dinner with Mr. Ansenjo. We had a very good conversation in Spanish. Mr. Ansenjo was a newspaper man and had to work nights. I got to bed about 1:30. At that hour, there were many people on the streets.

July 1st 1934 Sunday

Madrid, Spain

We got up late this morning. We had an appointment with Mr. Ansenjo at 11 so we went to a café and had breakfast. Our breakfast lasted from 11:15am to 2:30pm; that was why we sat there that long. He ate lunch with us. This afternoon, we went to the bullfight with Ernestro. It was not very good as the bulls were small and not good fighters. One bull hit a man and tossed him quite a way up in the air and he landed straight on its head. But the rest of the fighters distracted the bull from the man before the bull could get back to him. The fighter was not hurt badly but only knocked out. Plenty of horses were ruined today. Especially the one that was gored on the side where there was no padding.

Coming back, we passed the "Plaza de Alcala" and we could see where bullets had struck the arch (during the Napoleonic period) when strikes and the May riots took place. It was a favorite fighting spot for the people. I took a bath and went to bed early.

July 2nd 1934 Monday

Toledo, Spain

Last night, Mr. Brown had a very interesting talk with some men and they told him that they expected the government to fall today. A newspaper man told him the same thing.

We left for Toledo on the 9:20 train this morning with only our toothbrushes. On the train, we met the Toledo Rotary Club President and an army officer friend. It seemed much different to arrive and not have a few bands and a crowd of people to greet us. We walked to the city as opposed to the other time when we rode in high-powered cars. On the way to the hotel, we met several people that we knew. After dinner, we went to Rodriguez's office to see him about our pictures. We met Marianne Diaz and many others. We also met Perezagua on the street.

At night, we met the bunch at a café and then we went to the hotel where we had dinner for the commission of the two Toledos. There was Rodriquez, Adoracion Gomez Camarero, and Marianne Diaz. Perezagua came later and Fernando was not able to come. After dinner, we went back to the café and sat and talked. We did not get to bed until about 2am.

July 3rd 1934 Tuesday

Toledo, Spain

This morning, I did some shopping and I bought some gold work. I got two letters from home. I met a student friend and walked around with him after buying some wooden inlaid boxes. After I left him, I immediately met another student and we went to the Camarero Office and met Mr. Brown. We went to a café as we had invites for lunch at the Hotel Saining and Martin Gil.

After lunch, we went to De La Bander offices and had coffee. He had a very comfortable office. It had a radio and movie pictures machine. We saw movies of Corpus Christi Provencia from a few years ago. We also saw a picture of a bullfight. The picture showed the close calls that the bullfighters have. Then we walked around and visited, again for me but not for Mr. Brown as he was sick the time we visited, San Vicente museum, the home of El Greco (the painter) and a church where we saw Greco's greatest masterpiece. An artist was there making a copy; he had worked on the copy over a year and had to work for five months more before finishing it.

We visited the shop of Rodriguez. After getting some pictures, we returned to the hotel, had a rest, and wrote a lot of cards. While we were writing, the girl, Maria Luisa Aguado, with whom Bill was corresponding, called me by telephone and asked me to come to their home tonight. I thought I knew where they lived but after walking for 20 minutes through small and winding streets, I returned to the hotel and got a taxi.

We sat in their garden and talked. Their whole family was there, mother, daughter, and 2 sons. It was more or less a business talk as they wanted to know if ceramic work would sell in Toledo (Ohio). Camerero called by phone 3 times telling me to come as they were waiting for me to have dinner. The 2 brothers accompanied me there.

The Toledo commission sure is a swell bunch of fellows. There was Mr. Brown, Fernando, Rodriguez, Marianne Seinz, De la Bandera, Camarero, Perezagua, and me. We had a very nice dinner. We then went to the park and returned to the hotel where we bid farewell to the Toledo Spain Commission for the last time on this trip. We sure hated to leave each other as we had been such good friends. We went to bed at 2am. It was plenty hot.

July 4th 1934 Wednesday

Toledo to Madrid

We had to get up at 6am to catch the train for Madrid. I slept all the way. It was only a 2-hour run. We went to Hotel Sasi and washed up, had breakfast, and started right out as we had a lot to do. I went to the ABC to get some papers and the American Consulate but it was closed for the 4th of July.

After lunch, Mr. Brown showed me all the gold work he had bought and then we had a siesta. It rained a little. It is about the second time it has rained since we have been in Spain. I went afterward to buy some big combs and Mr.

Brown did other things. We arranged my passage this morning. It sure was hot!

Today after dinner, Mr. Brown went to say goodbye to his friends and I went to the Verbena with Ansenjo. The Verbena (a religious county fair overseen by the local virgin) was very big and we walked around and rode on a few things. We did a lot of shooting and I won quite a few prizes. I did not get back to the hotel until 2am.

July 5th 1934 Thursday

Madrid, Spain

This morning, we fixed my passage and then I went to scout headquarters but they were closed. I returned to the hotel and fixed all the newspapers we had. I also got a haircut and bought a suitcase. After dinner, I took a bath and then went to Café del Norte where I met Mr. Brown and some of the family with whom he had lived. They were Donna Antonia, Anita, and Paco. They were very nice.

I went to get our railroad tickets for tomorrow's train and I was at the end of the line with about 30 people. I stood in the wrong line at first. When I did get to the station, I found out that all the trains were loaded and we could not take the train we wanted. The first one we could get out of Madrid would be the seventh.

From there, we went to the American Embassy as guests of Mr. Bowers who had us for tea. We met their daughter and had a very nice talk with them. We then went back to the ticket office but it was closed. I got a streetcar and went to scout headquarters again as they told me that it was open from 7:30pm to 9:30pm. There I met the scout leader, district commissioner of scouts. A boy who could speak English guided me around. He sure was nice. He had been to the Jamborees in England and Hungary.

There were movies at their meeting. He explained to me about their scouting and showed me around. We had a very good conversation. He gave me one of their magazines. He accompanied me back to the hotel. Tonight I went to bed early as I was tired and Mr. Brown went out with Ernestro.

July 6th 1934 Friday

Madrid to Vitoria

We got our railroad tickets to leave on the extra train at 11:15pm. I went to the scout shop and bought some scout books. We went to the French, German, and American Consul for our French visas (transit) for 8 days, it cost 2.50 pesetas. The German visas were good for 3 months and cost Mr. Brown 6 pesetas. We then boarded the trains at the depot. All 3 classes were packed. Everybody was going north to get out of the heat of Madrid. We rode first class and sat up all night. It was cool riding on the train. We arrived in Vitoria at 9am.

July 7th 1934 Saturday

Vitoria, Spain

Mr. Erausquin's brother met us at the train station. We went to the hotel and got a swell room. It was the best one we had since we came to Spain. He came back for us at 11am and showed us around the town. He took us to the cathedral and showed us his new bank building where he worked. Then he ate dinner with us.

After dinner, I took a siesta as I was plenty tired. Mr. Brown and Mr. Erausquin went to the cemetery where Mr. Brown put some flowers on the graves of Mr. Erausquin's parents. I had a very good siesta and then went out and bought a Boina (Spanish beret).

We walked around and after dinner, we went to the park for a concert and got there in time for the last piece. We walked around some more and met Mr. Erausquin's brother again. We also met a man who could speak English. We talked to him for a while and he showed us a swell club. He said that he didn't know everybody in Vitoria but he assured us that everybody knew him. When we returned to the hotel, we did not go to bed but wrote cards till 1:30am. We wrote about 30 cards.

July 8th 1934 Sunday

Vitoria to San Sebastian

We got the 9am train out of Vitoria. We met an American woman in our compartment. It felt good to meet an American. We had a good conversation with her. We arrived at San Sebastian at 11:30am. All our baggage is a nuisance and it could be plenty for tips to porters. We went to the hotel, cleaned up, and wrote cards.

The air was very damp here.

They had a very wonderful and large beach. We drank a lot of Leche con cacao. We walked along the beach for about a mile or more. Mr. Brown almost fell in a pool as he slipped on some rocks. I fell and cut my hand. We walked along a boulevard near the ocean.

I saw the first drunk man that I had seen in Spain, or Europe for that matter. We stopped at a very good café to have seafood. When we returned to the hotel, we wrote some more cards, and ate. After dinner, we walked around the beach some more and stopped at a café. We brought two Leches con Cacao back to the hotel with us. We wrote more cards before going to bed.

July 9th 1934 Monday

San Sebastian to Irun to Paris

We got up at 7:30 as we were supposed to catch the morning train for Paris. The proprietors of the hotel took me to a shop and I bought 2 botijas (wineskins). I went to another small shop and bought two pairs of rope shoes. Mr. Brown got our railroad tickets but we were not to leave until the 3:30pm train because there were no third-class coaches on any train before then.

We walked around and tried to while away time until then. I got my last shoeshine in Spain. We got to our train and took our dinner with us. I had to carry my botijas in my hand. We were stopped and asked how many pesetas we were carrying out of Spain.

At Hendaya, France, we were stopped at customs. They searched our suitcases. They asked the head official about our gold-ware from Toledo, Spain, but we did not have to pay customs. We had to pay our fare twice as we got on the wrong train with our already bought tickets. We almost left our lunch on the train. We were going to Paris third-class and we had a compartment to ourselves. We left Hendaya at 6:47pm and arrived in Paris at 8am.

I put on my slippers and sweater and rode comfortably. We had a big dinner. Our train sure did go fast. I had the botijas fixed right between the suitcases. We rented some pillows, used the seats as beds and our overcoats as blankets. We slept pretty well. In Hendaya, I saw a toilet stool which had only 2 footmarks over a hole in the ground.

July 10th 1934 Tuesday

Paris, France

A French lineman met us on the train. He showed us to a very nice hotel. We went there, washed up and ate breakfast. Then we went to the French line and fixed my passage. Then to the American Express to cash some money. From there, we went to the American Embassy where I got a letter from home. We went to the Louvre and saw many famous and beautiful paintings. We then went to the Normandie Café which was near our "old" hotel, the Prince of Wales.

The Louvre sure was big and beautiful. While we were there, we saw the film "Wings of Victory" at the Normandie Theater. Then we had lunch. When we returned to the hotel, I found my bags. I had left them at the station. I wanted to open them up but I had lost my keys. One of Mr. Brown's keys opened the big suitcase. I borrowed some keys from the hotel but they wouldn't work either. I then went to a shop but they didn't speak English and didn't know what I wanted, even after I had shown them the key. I returned to the hotel and we had a siesta. I forced open the small cheap one to get to my things.

We walked down a small street which had a restaurant in every store. We stopped in one of them and had supper. It is a famous street because of the great number of restaurants. After dinner, we went to Champs Elysees and had coffee in one of the cafes. We sat there for quite a while and walked to the most famous café in Paris—Café La Paix. It is said that if you sit there, you will see everybody you know go by. We sat there awhile then returned to the hotel and went to bed.

July 11ᵗʰ 1934 Wednesday

Paris to Havre

After breakfast, we got the 10am train from Paris. Mr. Brown did not take any baggage. This will be the last break-up of the delegation. We arrived at Havre at 12:30pm. We took my baggage right on board the boat. Havre sure was a big port. Mr. Brown had to leave the boat at 1:45 as we sailed at 2. He sure had been a swell traveling companion. I wished he was going home with me.

After I could not see Mr. Brown anymore from the deck, I went below and ate. I had to get my suitcase open as I can't go to New York with only one shirt. I saw a movie this afternoon. We had another orchestra on board. After dinner, I went up and wrote in my diary and listened to the orchestra.

Then I walked around on deck. There was a very heavy fog as we were heading to Plymouth. The ship would blow its fog horn every few minutes and it sure was loud. We waited quite a while for the tender to come out and when it did come, we could not see it until it got very close to us. A little boat came first to let on a man who examined the people going ashore. The passengers came on board and the baggage was loaded. A car was loaded on the tender. I went to bed before the tender left.

July 12th 1934 Thursday

On board the "Paris"

After breakfast, I walked around on deck and played a game with some men on deck. It was throwing small disks for points. The disks had to go through a frog's mouth or some other holes. After dinner, I slept for a while and then worked on the other suitcase. I reached in the front part of it and pulled things out. It was tough on my hands, but at least I got my money belt out.

I saw more movies today. At dinner, some men sang some French songs and they sure could sing.

July 13th 1934 Friday

On board the "Paris"

This morning, I walked around the deck and met some orchestra fellows. They had gone to France for 4 days and were returning. We played ping-pong and that throwing game. Two of the orchestra fellows were seasick. We walked around the ship and saw third-class quarters. We went up in the bow of the ship. The wind was strong up there. The boat went through the water just as smooth as can be. We saw some fish jumping out of the water.

After dinner, I monkeyed around with the stamps I had gotten. I played ping-pong with one of the fellows and we went up to the bow of the ship again. I saw some more movies this afternoon. After dinner, I watched the races, listened to the orchestra, and went to bed. We got an extra hour of sleep as we had set our watches back an hour each day.

July 14th 1934 Saturday

On board the "Paris"

Today is a national holiday in France. Bastille Day. They had American, French, and Signal flags hanging on the ship. I monkeyed around again with my stamps and played ping-pong. After dinner, I laid on my bunk and fell asleep. There was a program of things today, a concert, a tournament, and some movies. It was quite foggy for a while this afternoon. I played ping-pong quite a lot and went to bed early.

July 15th 1934 Sunday

On board the "Paris"

I went to church this morning. Services were held in the grand salon. I saw more movies, played ping-pong and walked around the deck. I made out my declaration sheet today for customs. You have to declare everything you bought abroad.

Tonight it got rough and mist was coming on deck. It got quite rough during the night.

July 16th 1934 Monday

On board the "Paris"

We ran into a bad storm about midnight but I was asleep through it all as I had gone to bed early. Many had gotten sick who had never been seasick before. I remembered that I had woken up as I was going up and down in bed, but I thought we were rolling. Waves came way up on the decks, broke windows on the promenade deck, and bent and broke steel stairways. Water even entered staterooms through the portholes. I was told that on deck, chairs were sliding all over, waves were coming up high, and women were hysterical. At times, the propellers were even out of the water. Everybody was vomiting all over the decks. Many people were quite nervous, especially women.

This morning I saw them fixing the damaged things. We saw a three-masted sailboat off in the distance. I played more ping-pong and saw more movies today. Everybody was talking about the storm we had. There was going to be a performance tonight for sailors, widows, and orphans. Water that had entered the staterooms had soaked the beds and tossed baggage all around.

July 17th 1934

On board the "Paris"

I got up early this morning and saw a large swordfish jumping out of the water. I could see land at about 2pm. We could see Coney Island and the New York skyline quite easily. We stopped at the quarantine station for about an hour. A pilot was brought out to the boat and steered us in. It took quite a while to dock the boat.

I did not think that Dad and Mom would meet us but I saw Uncle Elmer and whistled at them. After Customs, we went to the hotel and then to dinner. Mom had eaten her first real meal in days as she had been sick. I opened my suitcases and showed them all of my gifts.

July 18th 1934 Wednesday

New York City

We got up early this morning and left for home. We tied the baggage on the back of the car. Our route home took us under the Hudson River. We traveled all day and stopped at Youngstown and Gettysburg. The mountains sure were high and there were plenty of curves in the roads. We went down plenty fast, freewheeling. One time, our brakes caught on fire as Uncle Elmer had pulled the emergency brake. We stopped at the tourist home.

July 19th 1934 Thursday

Gettysburg to Toledo

We rode again today and stopped at Youngstown. It was getting quite hot. We arrived home about 5pm and I was glad to arrive.

Time for Some More Context

After my grandfather returned from his trip to Spain, he went on to graduate from DeVilbiss High and then attended the University of Michigan where he went to medical school. It was at this time that he married my grandmother Betty and she became pregnant with my father. When she was 4 months pregnant with my father, my grandfather was drafted into World War 2.

Much like his journey to Spain a decade earlier, he also took this time to write down his experiences. Although there is a great introduction to the commissioned officers' first exposure to wartime, the breadth and scope of this second journal is not as extensive. Probably because of the violent warfare in the background and not the veiled references to civil war, like in the previous journal. Not as much time to reflect and the memories are a different kind of experiences.

Part 2
A Surgeon Goes to War

Personal Journal of Army Physician
George L. Schaiberger

May 22–August 2 1943

May 22

I went fishing with Dad this morning.

Betty and I left on the 6:46 pm train for Boston and Fort Devens. We both piled into an upper berth and had a fair night.

May 23

We pulled into Boston at 11 am and had breakfast on the train. We stopped by Betty's Uncle Erwin's and spent the day at Swampscott. Then we went down to the beach a couple of times.

May 24

I reported to Fort Devens and began filling out many papers. It was quite a busy day. The food was very good.

I obtained a room for Betty in Shirley, Mass. Just outside of camp.

Wow!—an officer—saluting and all…

The fort was very large; it will hold 90,000 men.

May 25

It was Betty's birthday today, her 21st. I was still doing so many things—reporting to officers and such. I had calisthenics at 6:30 am today, but we all got up at 5:30 by mistake. I had my vaccination today resulting in a sore arm which Betty certainly laid into.

We had drill today and we look just like a bunch of ducks.

Betty arrived at Shirley and proceeded to fall down the steps of the rooming house. She was a little bruised up, but she was fine. No baby issues.

May 26

Everybody who was at drill this morning was tired and sore. We were loosened up a little bit by calisthenics. We all saw "Desert Victory" again (winner of best documentary 1944 Academy Awards, TGS).

I met wounded boys for the first time this morning and now I am really aware of the hells of this war, boys with missing arms, legs, broken backs, and sometimes spines.

Betty came over for dinner tonight. She had gone shopping last night. We spent the evening at the officers' club. Betty can still beat me at ping-pong—2 out of 3 games.

There was a lull tonight and we didn't do much.

June 9

My left arm was very sore and I felt like the devil today although I still exercised and drilled. I was on the "alert" at 6 pm on Sunday.

I went to bed very early after calling home to Toledo.

June 10

I worked at the post hospital today. I felt better. Betty and I went to Watertown for dinner. We had a very good time and returned home all tired out.

June 11

We had the same old procedure at camp today.

Tonight the entire group had a dinner and party in Watertown. We all had a very good time dining, drinking, and singing.

Betty was beginning to get big, as she had to go upstairs right in the middle of the party and take off her girdle.

June 12

I got off at noon today. We went on a picnic to Sacket Harbor. We had a good time. I went swimming, but the water was too cold for Betty.

June 13

We loafed around all day and I packed up my things. I had to be at camp by 6 pm and Betty went into Watertown right away to stay with Helen as they were all leaving for New York in the morning.

June 14

I was cleared this morning with my 2nd tetanus shot. It was not as bad as the last one. I left Pine Camp at 5:30pm and we marched with full packs to the train. Train was hot and dirty as hell. Pulled down the seats and slept fairly well.

We all arrived at Camp Shanks, N.Y., at 5am and marched to our barracks which were not too hot. I slept most of the morning. I have heard a lot of rumors but few facts. I did nothing but lie around and eat. I wonder if Betty had arrived in N.Y. yet?

June 16

I wore coveralls in bed all night and slept like a log. I was to have an inspection this morning. After that, I gave typhus shots to all the men. Gave one poor devil, who didn't move out of line, 3 shots.

So far, no news is good news.

Laid around and slept all night through, again. We had a really big dinner. It was fair, but there was lots of it. After supper went to the show, drank 2 bottles of beer and had nothing to do again. It was really a very beautiful moon tonight. I will probably get to go to N.Y. city tomorrow night so I can see Betty.

June 17

I received heavily impregnated clothing that was issued at 11:30pm last night. It was all greasy and smelly. I helped censor mail this morning and really, really felt sorry for the boys—some of them at least. My friend Al said that the only piece of equipment that fit him was his necktie.

It was a tense moment when we drew for passes to go to N.Y. City. I got one and we left about 4:30pm and I got to Betty about 5:15. She was at Shelton's. We went to Zucco's for dinner and had a very large and delicious meal. Then we went to Macy's. We returned to our room and talked and…

Helen and Frank returned about 1 o'clock. Betty and I got another room so everyone could be alone and happy. Had to leave at 4:30am to get back to camp at 6am.

I said goodbye to Betty as I may not get back to NYC again. She was having a great time and really getting pregnant. She bought 2 maternity dresses. It was really wonderful to see her again.

June 18

I got in at camp at 6:00 and snoozed a few minutes before breakfast. We marched down to the gas chamber for a drill. It was for tear gas. Everyone argued a little about it, some more than others.

The gas exposure made my skin and moist areas burn like hell.

This evening we got ready to go to NYC. Lucked out on a pass again. While we were waiting for the bus to get us at

4:30pm, an MP came up and asked if we were of 2981 HH; we were on "alert" and had to return to quarters.

So I won't get to see Betty before leaving—damn it all. So we (Chet, Schaller, Frank, Coop, and I) went to a show and came back and packed our shoulder packs.

June 19

I woke up this morning and packages were at the foot of our beds from the girls—just like Christmas. Betty and Helen sent us cookies and cashmere sweaters. They certainly were swell sweaters! Also, there was a note from Betty saying she waited quite a while for me to come in... the ole' dear.

I understand from mail correspondence through Snooks Mill that Betty received $50.00 from Dad and didn't quite know what to do with it. I just wrote letters and loafed around all day. I went down to the O.C. (Officers Club) for beer and then home to bed.

My footlocker was all packed.

June 20

I got up early and rolled up my bedroll.

Everything we had was tagged for identification. Our 2 groups split up to go on different boats. Our footlockers and bedrolls were taken this morning.

It was going to be another scorcher today. I went to church and took communion. Loafed around this evening again and did a few odd jobs. I saw a baby with a soldier. It was the first time he saw his baby. His wife was at the gate and couldn't get in.

After supper, I went to the nurse's quarters and rolled bedrolls. It was really hot work, and sweaty. Came home and took shower in coveralls to wash them. I wrote a letter to Betty and then went to bed.

June 21

We vaccinated the rest of the nurses this morning. I washed my O.R. shirt, hoping it doesn't shrink. It is hot as hell today and the shirt dried swell, looking like it was ironed. This evening, we went swimming in 2 ole' mudholes. The water was dirty and smelly. We were afraid we might have gotten a sinus infection.

We ended up at a show tonight and then to bed.

June 22

I have been in the Army only 1 month today and leave tomorrow for England.

I was up at 6am as I always am as I still had things to do today. Some of the bags will probably leave today.

I lectured to a platoon on anatomy today and enjoyed it very much.

It was really very warm today.

Fanis, Valk, Rothrow, Chris, Cobe, McVay, Foerster, Padbug, and Jay left for the boat at 7pm in field jacket and full pack. The poor devils looked miserable as it was plenty hot. They marched down and we saw them off at the train. The nurses could hardly stand up under the weight of the pack.

O'Connor left at 5:30 in the morning and the rest of us tomorrow night. I ought to get a letter from Betty tomorrow—I hope so as I am really beginning to miss her.

Snooks and I exercised with the platoons this morning.

June 23

I loafed around all day and ate lunch at the cafeteria. Left the area with a full pack at 8:10pm and marched 20 minutes to the train. Not too warm.

I had weakness and slight palsy of my left arm due to the pressure on a nerve or loss of blood supply from the weight of the pack. The train left at 8:40pm. It had 3–4 seats. It was a half hour train ride.

We caught a ferry across the river and they guessed the ship to be the Queen Mary. Which it proved to be. There was a band and all of that at the dock. One hell of a job carrying the pack and also the Val A Pak. I was really pooped.

We do have a nice stateroom on the main deck in the center. There are 9 bunks in the room but also a toilet, bath, and 2 sinks. Really not bad at all.

We were all on board and settled by 10:30. The ship was really big and it will hold 16,000 men. It was well-armed too. I went to bed at midnight and really tried to sleep. I didn't and I was tired as hell. We took a saltwater bath and had only 2 meals a day. One at 7am and the other at 5pm. They produced 33,000 meals a day.

June 24

Up at 6:30am to eat at the first sitting at 7am. Good breakfast choices and plenty of it available, with waiters. I got the break of being assigned to a battle station which meant I could go up on deck during ARP (Air Raid Precautions) while the rest went down below. My assignment to the battle station put me just back of the last big guns.

There was a good opportunity at seeing action from this site but chances of seeing action were very poor as the ship had never been in any engagement. The only encounter it had had at all was about 6–9 months ago when it rammed one of its own destroyers, cutting it in two so that it sank in 30 seconds. No harm came to the Queen Mary at all.

Had a meeting this morning. The commander said that the ship was more important than any of the personnel.

I had ARP drill and as a hosting battle aid officer was able to be up on deck while all others were below. Enjoyed it very much. I saw the Statue of Liberty. We pressed through minefields and submarine nets. Blimps followed us for a while as well as airplanes. This ship traveled very fast and the sea was very calm. We went up toward Iceland and Norway and it got cold then. The decks, the holds, everywhere and everything, were teeming with men. With the packs and perspiration of these thousands of men, there was a heavy stench in the air.

I slept an hour and a half and then went down to D deck to get my men and show them our battle stations. I sat on the packed deck for a few hours and then went back down to quarters.

I took a bath and salt water was damn hard to work up a lather with. Had to wipe off all the dirt on a towel.

We had a fine dinner tonight consisting of roast duck.

We were headed for Scotland and north toward Iceland so it will get colder. Blackout at 5:30 as all were below decks then. Passed some fishing schooners late this night. Guess that's all for today.

June 25

Did nothing but loaf and sleep today and sit up on deck. A PBY plane (odd-looking Navy aircraft) flew around us many times at noon. Sleeping is just like being in a steam bath. Slept three and half hours in McGrath's bunk, which was cooler due to better ventilation.

Troops were certainly packed in. Crowding of Negroes reminded me of a slave ship. They certainly can harmonize.

June 26

It was getting much cooler as we must be going further north. I was at battle aid stations during drills this morning. I was located in the upper deck just behind the last stack and surrounded by 9.9 guns on deck just below and aft were 3" guns and Belgian guns.

Had quite a talk with a pleasant lieutenant (which is a captain in our forces). He made about 10 lbs. a week whereas I made 17 lbs. per week.

Have been thinking of Betty a lot so I better get busy doing something or I will be getting homesick.

Saw 2 water spouts made by a whale while on the deck after dinner. Also, I saw B-24s fly over and signal. Getting cooler and a little more roll-y. Played a little bridge in the lounge tonight. We had a band of enlisted men, they played pretty hot, the drummer was from Harry James' orchestra.

I played a little poker and won $1.50. I was up till 2am then to bed.

June 27

Up for breakfast and then back to bed for 2 hrs.

I got up and shaved. I'm starting a mustache. I washed my clothes in salt water, took a bath, then went up on deck for boat drill. I received a small packet from the Red Cross. It consisted of pencils, envelopes, pads, sewing kit, playing cards, and chewing gum.

This evening, I inoculated all our men with the typhus vaccine (180). It was getting much colder now. I slept a hell of a lot today. I read a book this evening while McGrath snored through the partitions.

June 28

I slept poorly again last night. After breakfast, I went up on deck but it was cold and raining so I went to bed and slept from 8:30am to 1:30pm. I had nothing to do. But I was better off than poor Schaller. His second wedding anniversary was today. Toasted him with water at dinner.

Everyone was certainly getting tired of eating Hershey's between meals.

I was up three dollars at poker after dinner. There was a show at 8pm—"Next of Kin". Not bad, following which the enlisted negro band played. They were pretty good. Seeing the movie and the band seemed more like I was at home and not on the ocean. Read until 2am. I certainly will be glad to get off this boat and finally have something to do.

June 29

Short nap this morning after breakfast. Due in Scotland (Glasgow) tonight. We were issued six cans of rations today. I was on deck and wrote a letter to Betty. About 1:30pm I saw Iceland. And also a convoy of about 18 ships. Very beautiful green hilly country going through the Firth of Clyde. Anchored at Firth about 8:30pm. A very safe quiet trip. 3 aircraft carriers and 3 catalinas in this natural harbor.

June 30

To bed about 2am and up at 4am for breakfast and then back to bed for catnaps. Left Queen Mary at 3pm on tender to Greenock. French cruisers were sunk in the Harbor. Masts were the only thing sticking out of the water. Left Greenock at 6pm on train.

First-class compartments for Bristol. The beautiful green rolling hills looked like patchwork quilts. Traveled through Scotland, saw many stone fences. Innumerable rabbits, Scottish castles, towns made up mostly of apartment houses. Brick or stone with red tile roofs. And small mounds like bomb shelters in the backyards.

Scottish soldiers were on the train with kilts, no underpants. I ate a couple of cans of rations; passed through the Glasgow shipyards with many ships in construction. Dinky little miniature boxcars. Beautiful evening and no dusk until midnight. Slept on the train stretched out on my seat—too much daydreaming. At Carlisle, England, I had a canteen cup of coffee. Just a week ago today, I had left Shanks, New Jersey. Only a month and a day after I had been in the Army, I sailed for England.

July 1

Arrived at Bristol at 7:15am. I saw a few bombed areas. We were met at the train by Colonel Keach and Colonel Maddock—their old professor of surgery. Our camp in hospital called Frenchy was about 7 miles from Bristol. A beautiful layout of all brick buildings. We met Towsley and others. They were all riding bicycles and glad to see us. I was a little homesick but it was going to be a nice setup here. Beautiful country and enough time off to get around.

Six of us had some beer before dinner. Not bad but it was flat. Powdered eggs for breakfast. Rounds of B&J with mac and cheese. A little of a good thing. I cabled Betty. 6 men to a quarters building. McGrath, Niell Farran, Schmale, Schaller.

July 2

Cold as hell to get up this morning in the galvanized and corrugated steel shack and had to run outside the dorm to the crapper. I was assigned to surgery this morning by Colonel Maddock. Scrubbed in with Thienne on a re-amputation of a thigh stump. Boy had both legs cut off. War is hell and a useless waste of life.

I helped with a cast. Helped Maddock and got to do the closure. Certainly felt good to get my hands in it again. Medical meeting this evening. I hope I can get a bicycle soon. Playing ball after dinner felt good but I sure was tired.

Appears that English girls have very loose morals. We had flowers on our stove today. Roses grow like weeds around here. Did dressings today. Really had the break to be over here. Only six weeks in the army and I was overseas, scrubbing in on operations.

July 3

I was assigned to the general surgery ward. We had a grounds inspection this morning. Grand ward rounds this evening in our blouses. Saw many interesting cases and really realized how fortunate I was to be here. Food was surprisingly good—chicken a la king and rice. Going to Bristol tonight. Saw really bombed areas and places really laid low; however, I was not impressed much; looked like old buildings had been laid low and torn down. But these people had gone through much and really deserved a lot of credit.

However, one wonders what for when one sees these young healthy boys with legs and arms off, blind, crippled, etc.

Bristol had narrow streets of old stone. I saw an abandoned cathedral. There was a barrage of bombers overhead. Went to the cinema—a good one. White women here dated negro soldiers. We went to a small pub. In fact, all of them were very small. Beer was warm and flat. And 13 cents for a small glass. Most of the English had a tooth missing. Just opened one of my ration cans for something to eat. A dog biscuit. Everything closed at 10 pm.

July 4

Good rolls for breakfast. Made rounds and then went to the chapel. All enlisted men called Frenchy "Little Ann Arbor". A very good dinner of steak, peas, and canned peaches. I saw 24 bombers flying toward France. I went for a bicycle ride, had supper, played ping-pong, and wrote letters.

July 5

I had three cases today and I was in the OR from 8 to 12:45 with finger amputations, hemorrhoid treatment, and a difficult closure of a colostomy. Had wards this evening and had very little to do. Did quite a large washing and scrubbed my beard. Played ball after dinner and had a swell time. We played against enlisted men. I took a shower and played ping-pong.

Had a couple of beers at the club. No drinks after 10 and only four drinks a day but all the beer and wine one wants. Got my ration card today. And it all had to be together for a week. It included 7 packages of cigarettes at 6 cents a package, 2 candy bars, 1 package of gum, 1 mint, 3 books of matches, 2 razor blades. I went back to my room and wrote letters. I'm really a letter writer now.

July 6

Removed pilonidal cyst this morning and had ward rounds. Had a nap in the early afternoon. But I was ready and present for inspection after dinner. What a farce. Movie, club, ping-pong, letters. The same thing every day. The rest of the group was arriving tomorrow. Read in the paper today about the planes I saw on Sunday had successfully bombed places in France on the Seine.

July 7

All set for inspection this morning by Major General Lee. He inspected our ward but I did not have to present the cases that I had memorized. Scrubbed in on an osteo of scapula and did an auxiliary abscess inspection. It was quite nuts. Another part of the unit arrived today. It was Farris, Volk, Rathburn, Paddery, Cooper, Jay, and Chris. Fourteen nurses and some enlisted men. I cycled over to the fish pond after dinner. Quite a time. Saw rows of stone houses and fences. Very cool evenings here.

I saw old houses, 800 years old. Saw groups of some guards about 12–17 years old, in uniforms with guns that they could hardly carry. They certainly could drill and march. Watched a boring cricket game and I needed two blankets tonight. Snook got a letter which raised his morale. Cold as hell to run down to the latrine to shower.

July 8

I bought a bike at Eastville. 9 lbs. 2 and a half shillings. A good buy. Rode it back and towed the one I rode earlier. It was quite a job getting up and down hills. About halfway back, I got a ride in one of our trucks. Went and saw a movie after dinner and washed my wool shirt. Got out my pack and slept with 3 blankets.

July 9

Watched two operations today. Had rounds, got a haircut, and went to a medical meeting. Saw the show "Air Free", played ping-pong, washed my hair, and wrote, then to bed. I also ironed my shirt, I did a fine job.

July 10

In ward this morning to prep for inspection. Slept two hours this afternoon. We got a new rug and the footlockers arrived and I was very glad to see them unpacked. I got out my pictures and things. I had to pay $123.00 dollars (30 lbs.). There was a dance in the Red Cross building. We had punch with ice, a banquet on ice. There were roses in the punch. McGrath left this evening for three weeks of field duty.

July 11

Worked at the ward. I am sweating a test on sepsis. I made a rack for my footlocker. I received the anxiously awaited letter from Betty. It rained all day and the weather was terrible. I went to chapel this evening.

July 12

We had been married 8 months today. I was in the operating room until 2pm. Queen Mary visited today. I went to Bristol tonight and did my washing. It rained off and on.

July 13

I was in the O.R. until 1am. A closure of a colostomy. Took a shower, worked a little, and played ping-pong. I did an appendectomy tonight. At 11pm did some washing, then went to bed at 1.

July 14

Worked in the ward today and gave a lecture. Examined men in the evening. Looked up all of 300 rectums. Caught a show tonight. It was bad for my morale. Herb had the radio working and it sounded swell. Had some trouble with the bicycle tire valve. Played a little tennis before dinner.

July 15

In the ward and worked in the O.P.D. Saw a change in the Colonel fellow. Taught two classes this evening. Got my bike fixed. USO show tonight. Very good. They had a swell contortionist.

July 16

I was in the O.R. until 2pm with a closure of a colostomy. Had a little drill. I had a medical meeting. Played tennis with Dan C. Pressed 3 pairs of pants. It was a really beautiful day. Heard the drone of many planes going out last night.

July 17

Worked in the ward. I had an inspection. Cycled quite a while after dinner. Took pictures. Stopped in a pub for a glass of cider. Awakened to hear about a friend going to Larden for six days of post-grad courses.

July 18

Verified and received orders to go to Larden for six days to the British post-grad medical school for a course on war surgery of extremities. Packed my bedding and 6 dollars a day for traveling. Telephoned for a room at Jules Hotel. I was at the American Red Cross Club. Left on the 12:30 train and arrived at Larden at 4:30. There were many munitions depots and an airfield very close by.

Jules Hotel was right off Piccadilly Circus. I ate at the club and walked around and first went out to Hammersmith Hospital by the OHS. It was in an interesting city, I saw many blitzed areas. I went to see a movie. And then to bed.

July 19

Out to Hammersmith at 4 am and had an M.C. staying here. D. Campbell of U of M. I registered for a fee of 1 guinea. I attended some very good lectures.

The lectures were from 10–4. Ate lunch at the hospital and then returned to the hotel. Went to Cheshire Chase and then to Wellington for dinner and then I walked around.

July 20

The lectures were quite good today except for x-ray. I slept a little, had a frugal lunch again, and went back to the Red Cross Club and got tickets for "Watch on the Rhine".

It started at 6:30 and was very good. Tea was served between acts. I had a photo taken to send home to Betty.

After the play, I went to a small French restaurant for dinner. Everything was expensive as hell. I walked home and wrote a letter to Betty. Showered and then to bed. Was hot as hell tonight.

July 21

I had lectures and saw proofs of surgery pictures today. Ate at the Red Cross Club. Had a good meal for 3 shillings. Went to bed early.

July 22

After lectures, I went to the Hippodrome to see "Lisbon Story". It had very good costumes, scenery, music, and the women were nice-looking. Went with Captains Farris, Rothburn, and Campbell. Went to the Savoy for dinner. Drinks were 1lb a round, 1lb for dinner. Baby chickens and a bottle of good wine. Walked down Piccadilly and then went to bed by 11.

July 23

Last of a lecture series today. It was a very good course. Got some pictures and they were fair. Ate at the Red Cross Club. We had a really good chicken. I took a walk to St. James park. There were shitter trenches in the park. Went to the newsreel movie and went home to bed. Packed 10lbs of spirit this week.

July 24

I took the train at 9am and the station was crowded as hell. Got to Bristol at 12 and rode to the hospital with a British major. Very nice of him to give us a ride. Saw a lot of bombed Bristol. 6 letters from Betty, it was certainly swell. Morale up 1000%. Ward round, did my washing, took a shower, and played tennis. I read the letters 3 more times.

July 25

Worked at the ward. Went to chapel, played tennis, and took a snooze. Received another letter from Betty. I went cycling.

July 26

Ward work, tennis, washed, not much to do.

July 27

Removed some shrapnel from a boy's tibia. Got a letter from Dad and Bob Perlberg. Saw a beautiful day rise up, played tennis, and saw a movie.

July 28

O.D. today. Worked in the ward. Boat crashed in the North Atlantic. Loss of bombardier and went down and crashed in the English channel. Fixed wounded legs. I saw a movie tonight and got a letter from Betty. Lonesome as hell.

July 29

Rounds at 9:30 and 12:30. Slept in the adjunct building. Bed was hard as hell. Heard gunfire (maybe a bomb?) about 12:30. I heard planes. It was a beautiful night.

Received three letters from Betty. They were quite welcome.

July 30

Up at 6. Did very little today; expecting another beautiful day. Did a little work in the ward. Talked to a first private who was all that survived in a crew of twenty. Shot through the shoulder as he was trying to get away from the truck and walked right into machine gunfire. I had 24 hours of RT.

Tennis this evening and softball after dinner. Took a shower, drank 2 beers, wrote letters to my dear, and then went to bed.

July 31

I was assigned to the B&J ward at 10 as a warrant officer. Will be glad to be busy. Got paid 144 dollars today. Bartended tonight and then saw a show. Went back home, washed, and showered. Then to bed.

August 1

I loafed around all day. At night, I worked in the ward. I definitely read a lot.

August 2

I removed ingrown nails this morning when I worked in the ward. Had a class and received three letters from Betty. Shocked at the death of Jack Cann. I played ball and went for a bike ride.

Journal Prologue

The 1943 journal ended with this entry. I don't know if he just stopped writing or maybe packed it away. I also believe that being in war might have taken away from his correspondence abilities. I don't know. But it was Nazis we were fighting.

The child that my grandmother had in her belly was my father. He would grow up the oldest of 6 brothers and would follow directly in his father's footsteps as a medical officer in the Army but would be deemed a combat medic.

The type of warfare being practiced during World War II was leagues apart from the guerilla warfare tactics of the NVA and Vietcong during the Vietnam war. There were no set, opposing lines, or standing armies. The Vietcong soldier or NVA regular could be dressed to look just like every other Vietnamese person. You never knew who was on your side. The concept that we shouldn't have really been involved in the first place really came to fruition after the release of the Pentagon Papers, but that is a story for another time.

This story is a remembrance of a tour of duty from 1967–68. The personalized recollection of my father's experience during one night of the Tet Offensive was accurately and thoroughly described the best he could.

Part 3
The Son Soon Follows

The following information is being copied by me for posterity. I am going to copy down word for word what was written. I will make any corrections in grammar and punctuation but I want everyone to know that this recollection is from my father and not me. I hope that you enjoy and appreciate what legacy I have chosen to live up to.

The following correspondence is from my father to my mother after the siege at Phu Loc in early 1968:

'Please read the letter first:

Darling,

This is my personally written account of all that occurred at Phu Loc. Don't read it unless you absolutely want to know all that happened in pretty much detail.

I Love You.

Also enclosed is the emergency medical treatment card filled out upon medical evacuation. Please save these documents, sweetheart, as they are quite vivid reminders of what happened.'

Recollection of SGT. E-5 George L. Schaiberger Jr.
7 January 1968

I was in bed asleep when an explosion occurred either in or immediately in front of our living quarters. I was thrown by the blast from my upper bunk underneath Major R.W. Cooper's which adjoined mine. I was immediately aware that we were under enemy attack, at this time I thought mortar. I attempted to find my glasses, M-2 carbine, and flak vest. My glasses and weapon were missing, probably due to the blast. I secured my protective gear and another pair of glasses from my wall locker. A .45 caliber automatic pistol was known by me to be hanging in a holster next to SP4 J.L. Tarbox's bunk. I procured the pistol and proceeded on my way to the bunker.

A blast in the hut knocked me rearward. I finally made it to the kitchen door where I noted CPT Winstead firing his M-16 from the rear door of the front bunker. Another blast just outside knocked me into the supply room adjoining the rear of the kitchen. I yelled to CPT Winstead that I was coming through to the bunker and immediately rushed to that location. Upon entering the bunker, I proceeded to the gun port where the .30 cal. machine gun was mounted. I commenced firing at ground level within my entire range of view, concentrating on the immediate inside perimeter since I now realized that the enemy were within the compound.

After what seemed to be a short period of firing the machine gun, a figure was noted at the far right side of my gun port. He immediately threw an explosive of some type into the bunker. I fled up to relative security at the rear of the bunker to join CPT Winstead. I yelled that they, the enemy, were all around and attempting to blow(sic) the bunkers. As soon as I reached CPT Winstead, the explosion occurred inside the bunker.

I then went back into the bunker and secured the BAR containing one full clip of ammunition. I then stood back to back with CPT Winstead and fired, mostly single shot since the weapon jammed repeatedly, around the bunker, in front of the hut, and even into the hut where I noted much movement and activity.

At this time, SP5 Branch and SP4 Tarbox entered our bunker from unknown locations. SP5 Branch had his .38 caliber revolver and commenced firing from the front of the bunker. SP4 Tarbox went inside the bunker with his weapon clutched to his chest, pleading with me to go aid Major Cooper in the CP bunker who was now injured. This action was forestalled by me because outside activity deemed it presently impossible. I slapped SP4 Tarbox on the face to rid him of what seemed mild hysteria and gave him the BAR. I also set up ammunition for the BAR and told him to aid CPT Winstead while I procured flares and grenades from inside the bunker.

Grenades were not to be found but I did get some flares out and then fired them from up on top near the rear door of the bunker. At this time, another violent explosion occurred inside the bunker and SP5 Branch emerged, dazed and seriously wounded. He refused any aid and began to fire his weapon from the rear of the bunker.

All of this time, mortars, small arms, grenades, and satchel charges were hitting all around us. SP5 Branch almost immediately was shot at point blank range with what I thought was an AK-47 rifle. He slumped to his knees and fell backward into my arms on the step of the bunker. I tried to get him out of danger and into the bunker. Just as I was pulling him into the bunker, he died. At this time, CPT Winstead and SP4 Tarbox departed enroute to the CP bunker, I think.

Also at the same time, an explosion occurred inside the bunker, hurling me against the outside wall. I hit this wall with my back, astride SP5 Branch's torso as debris from the roof and walls of the bunker began to bury me. CPT Winstead or SP4 Tarbox, I do not know which, returned to help me to the CP bunker. The vast amount of small arms fire and other explosions prevented any extensive effort and he was forced to withdraw. I was now trapped with just my head and right forearm exposed.

Ensuing explosions occurred, completely burying me except for a small air passage. I then proceeded to listen for the action and hope that my air supply would not diminish and that I would be dug out come daylight. The activity outside was one of continual explosions and small arms fire. I soon noticed that one of the enemy was on top of the debris on top of me, throwing explosive charges inside the bunker. I could not move and made no sound to give away my presence. Soon, another of the enemy came up yelling something and they both left.

I then tried, to no avail, to free myself with my relatively free right arm. Movement on my part caused more debris and dirt to come in on top of me. I then had to content myself to cover my face with my right hand to maintain breathing space and also keep burning metal and other hot debris away from my face. I know not long afterward, daylight was now in effect though, that I heard voices calling if anybody were in the bunker where I was entombed. After confirming the voices to be friendly, I responded.

Not soon after, I was elated to see that SPC Gibson and CPT Winstead, whom I both thought dead, were digging me out. With their help, I made it to the bunker's gun port and from there walked by myself to the established aid station in our helicopter landing zone.

I noted at this time extensive damage to the compound and two VC bodies. One body was near the trash cans and one near the front gate. Loss of my glasses restricted my noticing any particulars or details. At the aid station, a marine medic bandaged my head and the burns on my right hip. I lay down to cover myself with a blanket and attempt to warm myself. I soon left that position to see if anybody else needed help or medical advice. None was needed.

CPT Winstead and SPC Gibson were now at the aid station with me. We all awaited medical evacuation. A helicopter picked me up and flew us to the ARVN hospital in Hue. By asking questions and listening to others present, I was able to ascertain that Major Cooper and SP4 Tarbox were all right and had been evacuated.

During our wait for the helicopter evacuation, I noticed Sgt. Thai, our interpreter, to be completely free of any injury or dirt to be encountered in the fight that I presumed we had all just been through. He had spent the fight in the Vietnamese quarters so that SP5 Branch could sleep in the advisory team hut. Upon receiving later information, I learned that none of our defensive claymore mines or booby traps had been detonated. Does all of this lead to the suspicion on persons within our working area and sabotage?

Major Hahn, the district chief, was not even in the compound during the time of attack!

Upon our landing at the ARVN hospital, we were given some more first aid and partially cleaned up.

The ambulance from the MACV dispensary then came and we were soon given more extensive treatment. Later the same day, CPT Winstead, SPC Gibson, and I were taken to the Phu Bai hospital to have our ears checked for concussion injuries. We all had one or both eardrums ruptured. We then went to the Hue MACV compound to recuperate and await further action.

In reminiscing about the attack, I recall no or very little support from the Vietnamese on our side of the compound. I noted but one or two automatic weapons firing from the Vietnamese position on the hill to the left of the American portion of the compound. I also noticed a lack of hostile fire from any distance outside our perimeter. To my recollection, our 10kw generator also remained in operation during most of the attack. Why? The generator was finally shut off by SPC Gibson at 0630 hours.

*****

This was one of the most striking stories of the Vietnam War experience recalled by my father. His whole tour and war immersion was varied and wondrous, but this specific episode stayed with him always. The feeling of helplessness and betrayal influenced him the rest of his life. Unfortunately, my father died before he was able to properly recall his Vietnam War experience. He returned to Michigan after his tour ended and then my mother gave birth to my older brother. I came along around a decade after that.

Major Hahn, the district chief, was not even in the compound during the time of attack!

Upon our landing at the ARVN hospital, we were given some more first aid and partially cleaned up.

The ambulance from the MACV dispensary then came and we were soon given more extensive treatment. Later the same day, CPT Winstead, SPC Gibson, and I were taken to the Phu Bai hospital to have our ears checked for concussion injuries. We all had one or both eardrums ruptured. We then went to the Hue MACV compound to recuperate and await further action.

In reminiscing about the attack, I recall no or very little support from the Vietnamese on our side of the compound. I noted but one or two automatic weapons firing from the Vietnamese position on the hill to the left of the American portion of the compound. I also noticed a lack of hostile fire from any distance outside our perimeter. To my recollection, our 10kw generator also remained in operation during most of the attack. Why? The generator was finally shut off by SPC Gibson at 0630 hours.

*****

This was one of the most striking stories of the Vietnam War experience recalled by my father. His whole tour and war immersion was varied and wondrous, but this specific episode stayed with him always. The feeling of helplessness and betrayal influenced him the rest of his life. Unfortunately, my father died before he was able to properly recall his Vietnam War experience. He returned to Michigan after his tour ended and then my mother gave birth to my older brother. I came along around a decade after that.

References

According to the University of Toledo's website [*http://library.utoledo.edu/canaday/mssguide/mss-071.html*], the history of the Association of Two Toledos 'began in the 1920s when the University of Toledo President, Dr. Henry Doermann, visited Spain as an affiliate of the Royal Academy of Fine Arts and History in Toledo, Spain. [The photographs taken by Dr. Doermann of King Ferdinand and Queen Isabel's coat of arms inspired the University of Toledo's official seal.]'

'At the same time, Russell G.C. Brown, a Spanish teacher at Waite and DeVilbiss high schools, encouraged the students in his Spanish clubs to correspond with students studying English in Toledo, Spain. Doermann and Brown, together with people they had met in Toledo, Spain, formed the Committee on Relations with Toledo, Spain, in 1931. Dr. Doermann and Russell Brown led the organization in Toledo, Ohio, while Toledo, Spain's mayor, Guillermo Perezagua and Adoración Cómez Camarero, editor of the city's newspaper, led the organization in Toledo, Spain.'

'In 1934, a delegation was sent from Toledo, Ohio, to Toledo, Spain. "Fiesta Week" in Toledo, Ohio, corresponded with the trip. The celebration included an exhibition of Spanish art at the Toledo Museum of Art. A delegation from Toledo, Spain, planned to visit Ohio in 1937 to commemorate the 100th anniversary of the founding of Toledo, Ohio, but the Spanish Civil War in 1936 and World War II disrupted those plans.'

'The Committee remained inactive until 1958. However, informal communications were maintained between Russell Brown of the American committee and Pablo Rodríguez of the Spanish committee.'

'In 1962, a group from Toledo, Spain, visited Toledo, Ohio, as part of the celebration of Toledo, Ohio's 125-year history. In 1965, twenty-eight area high school students visited Toledo, Spain. A scholarship encouraging intercultural education was established in honor of Russell Brown in the late 1960s. A similar scholarship was established in Toledo, Spain, in 1971, thereby starting an exchange program. Awarding it the Town Affiliation Award in 1962 and an award for the "best people-to-people project' for fundraising to support the scholarship program.

'In 1976, a delegation from Toledo, Spain, again came to Toledo, Ohio, this time to celebrate the United States bicentennial. The two branches celebrated the 50th anniversary of their relationship in 1981 with a yearlong celebration in Toledo, Ohio. In 1982, the members voted to change the name of the organization from "Committee on Relations with Toledo, Spain" to "Association of Two Toledos". That same year, the Association sponsored an exhibit at the Toledo Museum of Art of works by El Greco.'

Special thanks to my uncle, Christopher Lowry Schaiberger, MD, F.A.C.S., for his biographical sketch of my grandfather.

Also, thank you to the most important men in my life, my father and grandfather, for their stories.

You will always be remembered.

Printed in the USA
CPSIA information can be obtained
at www.ICGtesting.com
LVHW021244310524
781674LV00012B/486